CROCHET MAKES FROM SCRAP CAKES

CROCHET MAKES FROM SCRAP CAKES

Turn your scrap yarn
into colourful
crochet projects

NAOMI VINCENT

DAVID & CHARLES
—PUBLISHING—

www.davidandcharles.com

CONTENTS

INTRODUCTION **6**

Tools & Materials 8

Abbreviations 10

WHAT IS A SCRAP CAKE **12**

Getting Started 14

Creating a Colourway 18

Arm Spans 22

Magic Knots 24

Yarn Winders 26

Scrap Cakes for Universal Projects 28

THE PROJECTS **30**

Sarah's Snood 32

Hessian Bag Cover 36

Sunshine Wrap 40

Tulip Tote Bag 46

Triangle Puff Shawl 50

Dave's Blanket 54

Corner to Corner Blanket 58

Pisa Cowl 62

Granny Square Blanket 66

Pot Cover 70

Clutch Bag 74

Balloon Pillow 80

Moss Stitch Blanket 84

Basket Set 88

Hexagon Cardigan 92

GENERAL TECHNIQUES 100

Magic Ring 102

Chainless Foundation 103

Other Stitches 105

Square Variations 108

ABOUT THE AUTHOR & ACKNOWLEDGEMENTS 110

INDEX 111

INTRODUCTION

I bet you have a great stash of leftover yarns and but none are enough to make something new? Let's make something fabulous with all those leftover yarns! From blankets to baskets, bags to shawls – any project can be a scrappy project!

Within this book, I will help you to understand how to make a scrap cake for a project of your choice and how to measure your yarn scraps to make it work. Making scrap cakes for projects is an excellent way to use up and reuse all your scraps to prevent waste and clear up some space! It lets us create useful items or garments from things we would normally hoard or throw away.

Each pattern in this book will have the scrap cake measurements at the start but if you do prefer to create your own pattern, you need to think about how you want the colours to change throughout the design.

For my scrap cakes and colour combinations I take inspiration from everything I see around me, mostly scenery, textiles and food. My favourite colourways to create are the four seasons. My favourite is autumn made up of warming earthy tones and khaki greens.

Sticking to a particular theme or subject when creating your colourway will give the finished look a more polished look and more significant and with personal meaning to you.

My personal recommendation is also to invest in a yarn winder! These contraptions will change the way you wind your yarn forever more. They are definitely the saviour of all scrap yarn stashes and a must have for any yarn-y crafter.

Now onto the yarn stash itself. I prefer to organise by scrap stash depending on how much yarn is left of each type. Once I've wound the yarn, I label each yarn cake with its weight.

Of course, you can sort your scraps by colour as well, especially if you have specific colour combinations in mind! I personally like to keep them separated by weight and worry about colours matching later. I also love a random colour mix where I don't worry too much about shades or tones matching in advance.

Have a look through my patterns within this book or create a new pattern of your choice; either way let's get the yarn measurements for your pattern started!

TOOLS & MATERIALS

You will need a few simple tools and materials to make your scrap cakes and crochet your projects. This list will give you an overview of everything that will come in useful, starting with the most important: hooks and yarn.

CROCHET HOOKS

Use your favourite type of hook for the projects in this book. Depending on your grip, you may prefer an ergonomic handle. Also consider if metal or wooden hooks work best for you. While wooden hooks are a bit more grippy, which is useful for slippy yarns like acrylic, metal hooks are cheap and light weight.

You will need a range of sizes from 4mm (US G-6) to 7mm (K-10.5 or L-11) crochet hooks. Always check your gauge and adjust your hook size accordingly.

YARN

Your scrap yarns will be your most important material. You can use whatever colours you like (see Creating a Colourway). DK weight yarn is used throughout and will be easiest to make gauge. All samples were made using acrylic or an acrylic cotton mix, however you can used whichever yarn you prefer gives you gauge.

MEASURING TAPE

A measuring tape is essential for making sure your lengths of scrap yarn are about the right size. The most important lengths you will measure are between 50cm (20in) and 178cm (70in), so make sure your measuring tape is long enough.

WEIGHING SCALES

Weighing your yarn is the easiest way to make sure you have enough yarn for your project.

You will need to weigh yarn amounts between 50g (1¾oz) and 200g (7oz) so you can use your regular kitchen scales to weigh your scrap cakes.

SCISSORS

You will need to cut your yarn to measure the correct lengths for your scrap cakes, so keep a pair of scissors close by!

As you will need to cut the yarn close to the magic knots, a small, sharp pair of scissors like embroidery scissors are easiest to use.

DARNING/TAPESTRY NEEDLE

The beauty of scrap cakes is that you will have only a few ends to weave in, but there will be at least the starting and end tails left. You will need a suitable needle to finish weaving these in. Tapestry needles are blunt and easy to use with a large eye to thread your yarn.

POMPOM MAKER

Pompoms are fun embellishments for the edges of shawls or blankets and add a extra layer of whimsy. Pompom makers are available in a range of sizes and make the job easy, but you can just use the cardboard ring method as well.

STITCH MARKERS

When working on your projects, there will be times you want to identify stitches for future rounds. This includes the beginning of the round, or stitches that are otherwise tricky to see. Locking stitch markers come in a variety of designs from basic to beautiful and intricate. However, a scrap piece of different coloured yarn or a safety pin will work just as well.

YARN WINDER

A yarn winder is an amazing tool to help you create neat cakes of yarn and make the process of winding scrap cakes easier. A cake of yarn is easier to work with, allows you to work with a centre pull to keep your yarn neat and helps keep your yarn stash tidy.

YARN BOWL

A yarn bowl is a medium sized bowl with a swirl opening on one side to feed your yarn through. Keeping your yarn contained in the bowl will stop it from rolling away while you work which can make crocheting more comfortable. It can also help keep your tension (gauge) even if that is something you struggle with.

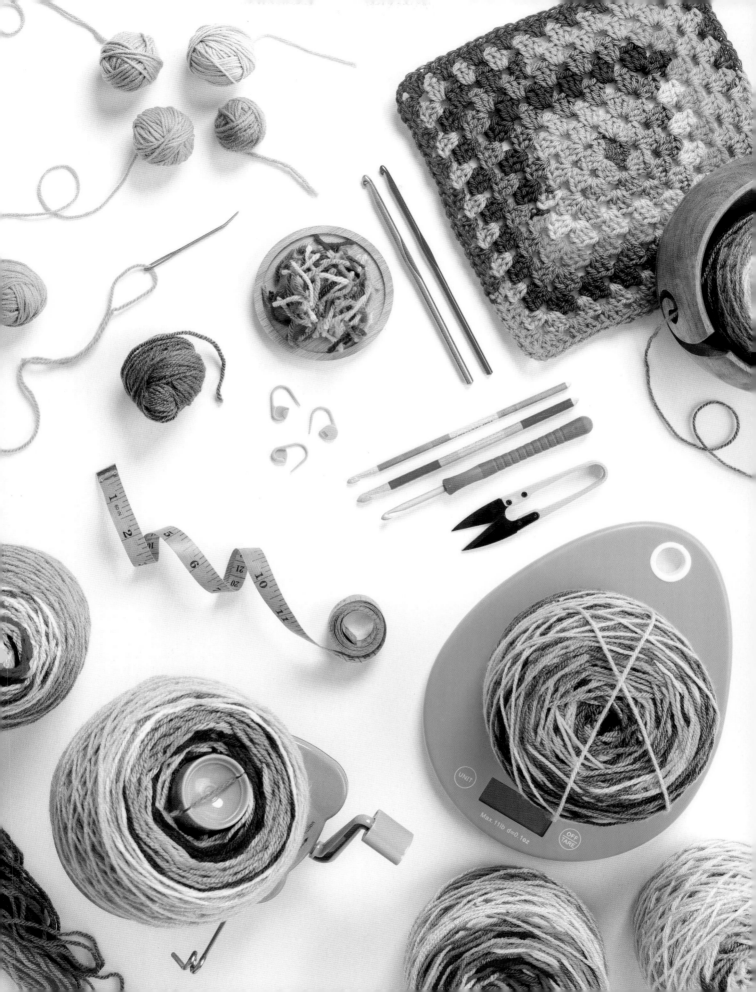

ABBREVIATIONS

This book is written using US crochet terms. Please refer to the tables below for the abbreviations used and conversions for US/UK crochet terms and US/metric hook sizes.

*	repeat the instructions following the single asterisk as directed until the following * to close the sequence.
( )	work instructions within the brackets as many times as directed.
alt	alternate
as	arm span
bl	back loop
BP	back post
ch	chain
ch-sp	chain space
cl	cluster stitch
dc	double crochet
dc2tog	double crochet two stitches together
dtr	double treble
FP	front post
hdc	half double crochet
mr	magic ring
ps	puff stitch
RS	right side
sc	single rochet
slst	slip stitch
st	stitch
stsc	stacked single crochet
sttr	stacked treble
tr	treble crochet
WS	wrong side
yo	yarn over

UK to US Crochet Terms

US Terms	UK Terms
Single crochet (sc)	Double crochet
Half double crochet (hdc)	Half treble crochet
Double crochet (dc)	Treble crochet
Treble crochet (tr)	Double treble crochet

Hook size conversions

Metric Size	US Hook Size
4mm	G-6
4.5mm	7
5mm	H-8
6mm	J-10
6.5mm	K-10.5
7mm	K-10.5 or L-11

What is a SCRAP CAKE?

Scrap cakes are a way of creating a custom colourway by knotting together all the unused scraps of yarn that have accumulated over time. Scrap cakes can reduce the amount of waste left from other projects, eliminate the need to weave in ends on multicolour projects and provide a new perspective on colour combinations.

Scrap cakes are the answer for that pile of partially used skeins (hanks) and scraps that accumulates for all of us. This sometimes tangled mess can be quite daunting, but organising your yarn into scrap cakes can provide new joy and endless possibilities.

A scrap cake can be a simple creation using all the colours in your collection, whether they match or not, or you can create the perfect colourway for a project to match the finished objects the scraps originally came from. If you're after the random Boho scrappy look, or a fun and sporadic colourway, scrap cakes are the perfect option.

Once you have made one scrap cake, the possibilities are endless for many many more projects with the scrappy look!

GETTING STARTED

Firstly, sort and organise your scrap collection (or in my case my scrap hoard!). You could use a selection of small baskets or boxes to keep your collection arranged by amount or colour. You can either weigh your amounts using a set of scales or note down the arm span (AS) measurements (see Magic Knots and Arm Spans).

I recommend making labels using scraps of cards (I like to cut up pretty birthday cards) to make a note of what each scrap is. Tie the label to the end of the yarn's tail. For balled up yarns, tie your piece of card securely and slip stitch the tail to the side to stop it unravelling.

Secondly, before you dive into cutting or tying anything at all, you need to know what pattern you going to make. Every project has its starting point and each stitch uses a different amount of yarn. If you are using all single crochet, you will use less yarn than if you are using all double crochet, as double crochet would use approximately twice the amount. Other stitches like a puff stitch or popcorn stitch are even larger. As these stitches use up so much more yarn than double or single crochet stitches, each scrap would need to be even longer.

The way your project is worked up will determine how your lengths are measured. Here are two examples to show how you might go about this, but don't worry – each project in the book comes with full instructions on what scrap lengths you need.

For extra projects, why not just make up a random length scrap cake? A lottery cake! Anything is possible! Mixed lengths and random colours can be so much more fun and great to work up in any project! Yes, any – short or long projects, granny squares, row by row – the rules are for breaking, so why not just have some fun with it? Plus the effects are surprisingly appealing too.

I also advise that when you are working from your pre-made scrap cake and you find a point in the project that the colours aren't building the way you would like, then you can simply cut the yarn. You can either remove some colours you don't like or add some new colours you do like. It's your call! Adjustments or rearranging are all part of creation and design.

Notes

For scrap cakes, I prefer using only acrylic or cotton mixed yarns. However, you can use any scraps you like as long as they match in yarn weight and will tie into a secure magic knot (see Magic Knots). Give it a try on some scraps before you commit.

Note that different yarn compositions may have a different metreage/yardage per weight, so the amount you need may vary. The projects in this book are made using acrylic yarns only.

HINTS AND TIPS

When cutting your yarns

Have a good tape measure! If you have a good sized workspace, you can use adhesive putty or tape to secure the beginning end of your tape to one end of the table then unroll it over the length of your table and stick it down on the other side too. This stays stuck to my table until I've finished measuring my patterns. When measuring the yarn length, I place the end on the start with a little adhesive putty to hold it in place, work the yarn up to the measurement needed and cut. Do not pull the yarn too tight. Let it relax as this gives a truer measurement.

Another trick is that if a measurement states *4AS + 114.5cm (45in) then start with the 45in first. Place the end of the yarn on the beginning of the tape measure, work the yarn up to the 114.5cm (45in), place your palm after the 114.5cm (45in). Hold the yarn here to measure the 4 AS (see Magic Knots and Arm Spans).

Don't forget that if you have a large bulk of the same colour yarn, you can always cut it up to make it spread across different projects or you can use it scattered across the same project.

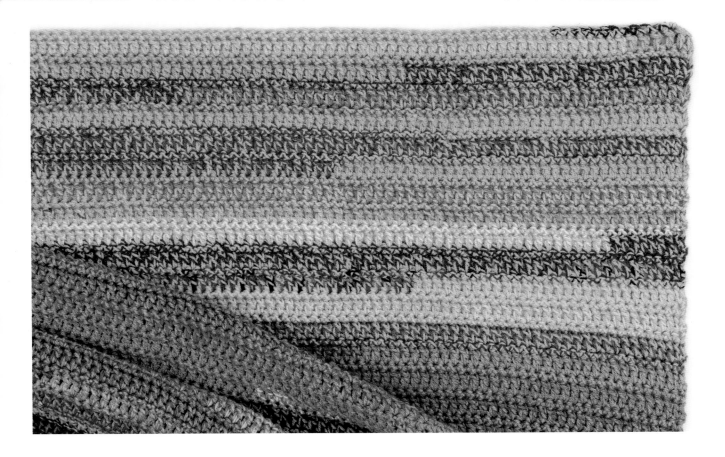

EXAMPLE ONE

The easiest example is a blanket worked row by row with all rows the same length. This means most of your scraps will need to be roughly the same length too.

Start by making a chainless foundation (see General Techniques: Chainless Foundation) to measure how much yarn you will need per row on your blanket. Make sure you base it on the stitch you are planning to use in your project.

Once you have made your foundation row, unravel it and note your desired length and the stitch count you used for future reference. Cut your yarn at this length.

To use this length of yarn as your guide, weigh it, measure it or use the AS technique (see Arm Spans). Remember you do not have to be totally precise. It's a scrap project so go rogue! Then cut your other lengths of scrap yarn to match and work up a good pile of mixed colours to your choice of colour palette.

To avoid the colour change always being at the start of the row, use a shorter length as your first scrap. That way, the colour change can happen somewhere in the middle of the row.

I also like to add a few random shorter lengths, say every 20 lengths or so, just to break up the flow of the changeover. When working row by row the colour change can end up at the same point every row, so having a random shorter length thrown in can rejig the rhythm up to keep that sporadic look. Plus it can be a random brighter colour to add a pop of extra contrast!

When arranging the rhythm of colour, it helps to include neutrals in between the brights and avoid placing similar colours too close together. Arranging them on a table (or even the floor!) is the perfect way to visually see the colour arrangement.

Once you have decided your colour arrangement you can start joining your scraps together using the Magic Knot (see Magic Knots and Arm Spans).

A blanket can use from less than 500g (17¾oz) of DK weight yarn for a baby blanket to over a 1kg (35¼oz) of yarn for a full sized blanket, so collecting this many scraps can definitely be a challenge. However, it can become your go-to blanket that you add to over time each time you have collected a certain number of scraps.

EXAMPLE TWO

If my project started small and the rows grew longer, like a triangle or circle, we need to measure our lengths from short to long.

Start by working your first few rows, changing colours around 3 stitches before the end of the row/round. Each time, cut your yarn and tie your next yarn choice to the end before working the next row.

After you have worked up at least 15 rows/rounds, count how many stitches that last row/round has and make a note. Unravel the last row/round and measure its lengths. Note down the last length measurement next to the stitch count you made. Now you can work out how much length each stitch will take.

Knowing how much yarn each stitch requires helps you work out how much yarn each row/round of your work will take. To make building your scrap cake easier, you can work out the length every 10–20 rows/rounds. Remember to add in a few shorter length to keep the location of the colour change more random.

CREATING A COLOURWAY

There are many ways to sort your yarn stash to create gorgeous colourways. Here are a few ideas to get you started.

USE THE COLOUR WHEEL

My favourite colour palette has to be "boho", a Bohemian array of offset colour. Take the colour wheel with its primary colours and off-set them slightly; this will give you a much deeper, smoother, softer, or warmer shade compared to the primary colour. Combine several such variations for a great "boho" colourway. This includes colours like mustards, olives, petrol or denim blue, duck egg blues, peachy pinks, minty greens, lime green, warming lilacs, rusty browns or deep oranges.

GROUP YOUR SCRAPS

If you are working from a pile of your leftovers, this can mean you have a small amount of colours and maybe a lot of whites, greys and creams. This can be a great thing! You can build your scrap cakes colourway with these lighter shades in between the colours, using the bright colours to break up the neutrals.

If you have a mass amount of yarn that seems overwhelming, break it up into groups. Have a pile that's all earthy tones, a pile that is all rainbow tones, and one that is all the odds. You could find a scenic photo you love and try to match your yarns to the photo's palette. Try a digital effect that blurs the picture to help you focus on just the colours.

MAKE A SWATCH

What if your leftovers are a variety of colours you think 'just don't match?' Give it go by making a swatch. Cut 1 AS of each colour, fold the lengths neatly and arrange in the order you think works best – even if you're not sure if it is perfect. Start joining them and if you realise that the next one you have lined up might not be right, don't hesitate to switch it up. You can be adventurous; blue can go next to pink and orange, and you can even put two greens next to each other, especially if they're totally different shades. There are no rules!

Once you have caked up 30g (1oz) or so, start making a little swatch. I like to use the moss stitch for a quick sample swatch to see if the colours work well together. This way you can see whether all the colours are happy together or if maybe that one dark navy one just doesn't get on well with the others. Now you know what works and can make your final scrap cake accordingly.

CHOOSE A CONTRAST SHADE

Another great way of figuring out a colour scheme is to just grab a yarn isn't classed as scraps and use this as an accent or contrast shade. This can then be your go-to colour for all colour palettes. Mine is a biscuit shade or a mustard. Then you can pick any scraps that go well with this colour. Use it as a yarn held double for a heavy blanket or as a contrast shade to surround bright, scrappy pops of colour on a shawl.

CHOOSE A THEME

For fun colourway ideas, I have used a selection of different groups of fun palettes for many years that help when picking what's your go-to colourway. Fan of the 90's? Go for a neon mix, throw in a bright yellow, a vibrant navy or a hot fuchsia to break up the neon. I also like to include white with neon, it makes the colours stand out even more!

Maybe going for a full rainbow colourway is your favourite? Try adding a hot mustard or foxy brown to the mix.

If you prefer a more monochrome blend, there are many fabulous greys with speckles that would work up great alongside each other and mixed with some blacks and whites. I also like to add in a textured or mixed dyed neon yarn into the monochrome to give it a tiny burst of colour.

I also love to make up a colourway to match the seasons. Autumn is my favourite and often use mustards, browns, oranges, with a tiny few moss greens worked in to break up the orange flow.

Winter would be a great cool colourway, would you go for all blends of blues and mints or would icy whites and shiny reflective greys be your kind of winter? Adding darker navy or deep turquoise would be a great contrast shade.

Summer and spring are very similar when working up a colourway. I like to add more luscious greens to spring, and more blues and purple tones for summer. Both can reflect the colours of the flowers that are your favourites for spring or summer.

USE A PHOTO

Just for this book, I have created a new colourway that reflects a pebble beach. We were out for a late summer walk on the beach and I stopped to take a photo of the pebbles because we all do that right? I noticed the different tones and colours that built up the natural shade we see on the beach. With this photo I used an app on my phone to create the blurry effect, this way I can focus on the colours more. Luckily, I found many of them in my yarn stash! So I built up a swatch on some card by wrapping small lengths around a bookmark shaped piece, cut out of a cardboard box, and created a beautiful collection of pebble tones.

Maybe you have a favourite holiday memory or a place you love to visit that has a beautiful view or scenic garden. Take a picture and use that photo to create your colourway. The woods with the sun setting through the trees or a field full of greens or browns to show the seasons? A view of the sea and the skies with a sandy beach? Your favourite childhood garden? Any photo that makes you smile will do! Play around with the blurring effect or use an artist app to create the palette of different colours in that image.

ARM SPANS

When measuring the lengths of scrap yarn, getting the tape measurer out each time can be an awkward hassle. Instead, we can use the span of our arms as a measurement. An arm span is the distance between your hands when spreading your arms wide, it is the easiest way to quickly measure your scraps.

WHAT IS AN ARM SPAN?

This is exactly what it means: the span of your arms as a single measurement! Hold your arms out like you are flying – hand to hand this is your new measuring device. My arm span (AS) is 160cm (63in).

Measure your own arm span by holding the end of the yarn in a clenched fist and work the other hand along the length until your arms are stretched out wide. Hold tight to that part of yarn and you can now let go of the first end. Cut the yarn at your second hand and measure the length. This is your own AS/arm span measurement. Use this measurement throughout the book as your guide, written as AS from here on. For example, some measurements will state "2AS + 76cm (30in)".

To make your life easier, notice how 76cm (30in) is about half my AS. Therefore, you can measure the yarn from your clenched fist stretched out to the centre of your chest and cut there to get your half AS, or roughly 76cm (30in).

When measuring the particularly long lengths I always find it best to neatly fold them into loops after cutting. Hold both ends together and fold the remainder up into loops, to have it ready and tangle free. When it needs to be joined to its neighbours, the ends are ready to grab (A)!

When a pattern calls for many of the same lengths, measure each one separately and place them on a work surface neatly, you can then arrange them into the colour sequence you like. Moving similar colours apart from each other (B).

If you are limited in how you are able to spread your arms out sideways. Use a 12.5cm (5in) square piece of card (cut two and tape them together to give it extra strength). Wrap your yarn around the square continuously counting each wrap as you go. This can be your measurement guide. For example, 1AS = 7 wraps and 76cm (30in) = 3 wraps.

Remember to weigh your finished scrap cakes to make sure they match the given weights as AS can vary between people. This won't affect the scrappy look of your projects as long as your total amount of yarn is correct. Adjust by adding more or fewer lengths to your final scrap cakes.

MEASURING SCRAPS FOR A PROJECT

In this book, each project includes a table with all the measurements needed for the scrap cake(s). Here is an example that is taken from the Sunshine Wrap.

You will have already chosen a pile of DK (light worsted) weight scraps in the colours of your choice. There are no colours given for the projects, these will depend on what scraps you have at hand and your choices (see Creating a Colourway).

The first thing to note is the name and total weight of the scrap cake – Yarn 1: 35g (1¾oz) Scrap cake. Not all scrap cakes have a name, only those where there are more than one scrap cake used in the pattern. The weight of the total scrap cake will be 35g (1¾oz).

Then, start by measuring your lengths. The first length is 50cm (20in). Then, you will need two lengths each measuring 100cm (40in). Make sure you keep them in the right order – I prefer knotting them together straight away, so they don't get mixed up! (See Magic Knots).

Yarn 1: 35g (1¾oz) Scrap cake
1 x 50cm (20in)
2 x 100cm (40in)
1 x 1 AS
1 x 2 AS
20 x 1 to 3 AS

Keep going down the table: one length measuring 1 AS, then one length measuring 2 AS. Finally you will need twenty lengths measuring somewhere between 1 and 3 AS each. You can play around a bit here, use longer lengths of your favourite colours or just go along with the scrap lengths you have!

Once you have finished measuring and knotting all your lengths together (again, make sure you kept them in the right order!), wind them into a yarn cake (see Using a Yarn Winder). Then, weigh your yarn cake. If it is 35g (1¾oz) or more, you are ready to start crocheting. If not, just add a few more lengths of scrap yarn, using the last measurement on the table, until you reach the weight you need.

When you start crocheting, make sure you start with the end from the beginning of the table. If you wind your scrap cake as you are making it, this will be the centre pull.

A

B

MAGIC KNOTS

The magic knot technique is the best and most efficient method to use for building your scrap cakes. This technique, once practised, is the quickest and easiest way to join your yarns together and once mastered you will not look back (or rather, only with the knowledge of how much time you could have saved on if you had learned it sooner, I know I did!).

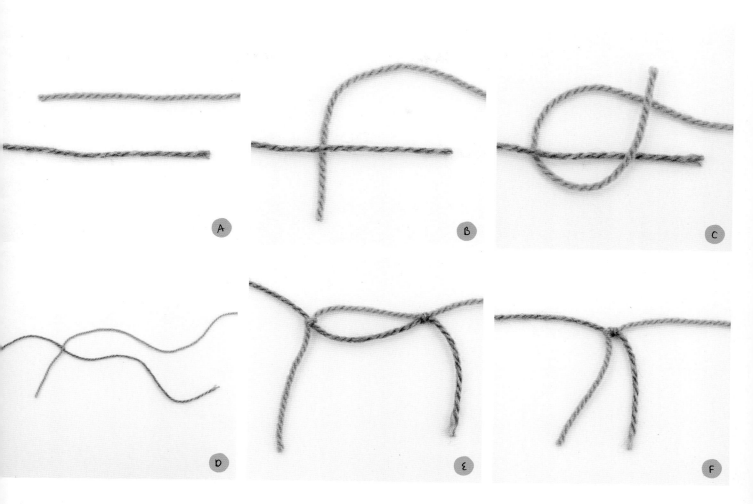

Place your two yarns on a flat surface with each going in opposite directions with about a 12.5cm (5in) overlap (A). Tie the top yarn to the lower yarn about 12.5cm (5in) from the end with a simple knot leaving a rough 2.5cm (1in) tail (B–D). Now tie the lower yarn end to the top yarn, (again 12.5cm/5in from the end) with a simple knot, again leaving a rough 2.5cm (1in) tail (E).

Once both knots are tied, pull on the long ends of both yarn so the knots join up in the middle. Holding both yarns in one hand, give the short tails a further pull to tighten them (F). Carefully cut the tails as close to the knot as you can.

Nowpullbothyarnshardtotesttheknot. 99% of the time they will be perfectly tight! 1% of the time it might come undone but you can just redo it again. Don't worry about losing that short length off the measurements.

Notes

It was a member of a crocheting group years and years ago, who, on seeing all the ends yet to be woven in on my first scrappy blanket, told me "OMG, all those ends! Haven't you ever heard of a magic knot?!" So I learned the Magic Knot straight away and it honestly changed everything for me. So my scrap cake building world began.

YARN WINDERS

Once you've chosen your colour scheme and joined your lengths of yarn together, it's time to make your scrap cake. That's where your yarn winder comes in. A yarn winder is an amazing tool that helps you create neat cakes of yarn. Winders can be temperamental, but with practice they can also be amazing fun, and you will find yourself winding every skein you buy. So they are definitely worth the purchase. So go for it – wind up your scrap cakes!

PREPARING A YARN WINDER

When attaching the winder to a table – for example your precious wooden dining table! – you can use a scrap piece of card to sit under the screw that tightens against the surface to protect your table. You can also use a ball of adhesive putty to hold the arm upright, this helps to stop it falling when winding. When I am winding on my yarn, I pause every now and then to give the cake a little squeeze. This helps fit more yarn onto the cake. I have found my yarn winder isn't great with weights higher than 150g (5¼oz) so I tend to squeeze the bulk on the winder to fit it all on neatly. This also helps with the winding flow, sometimes I find it flies off the top or drops to the bottom before the bottom reaches the little platform edge.

USING A YARN WINDER

A yarn winder is a great tool to have in your craft collection. It is definitely one of those tools that I think are worth investing in. It is fairly small and can be attached to any table – your desk, your dining table or even a kitchen worktop.

Step 1: Attach your yarn winder to a solid surface. If you are worried about scratching the surface, place a piece of card or fabric on each side between the yarn winder and your table surface.

Tip: Before you start, remove the spool and weigh it. This will make checking the weight of your yarn cake much easier.

Step 2: Feed the yarn through the metal arm and attach the end to the top notch in the central spool (A).

Important: Attach the end of the yarn you will start working with as you will be making a centre pull cake. For the patterns in this book, that means start with the yarn lengths at the top of the list.

Step 3: Holding the yarn at a slight tension, start turning the arm gently to wind the yarn. The loose end at the top of the spool will be caught underneath subsequent rotations, securing it in place. Once your yarn is wound around the spool several times and feels secure, you can start to speed up (B).

Tip: If the yarn tangles before meeting the winder, go more slowly or stop and gently untangle it before continuing. Practise makes perfect!

Tip: If your yarn winder is becoming quite full before you are quite finished, you can often squeeze on some more yarn by gently squeezing the cake on the spool to reduce its size. If you still have a lot of yarn to wind, split it into two cakes – just make sure to label which one is which so you use them in the

Step 4: Once you have all your yarn on the yarn winder, you are ready to remove the spool. Make sure no yarn is wound too tightly and trapped underneath the spool. If it is, gently push it back up onto the spool. Then, remove the spool from the yarn winder.

Tip: You can weigh your yarn cake together with the spool to check if you have reached the correct weight. Simply weigh them and subtract the weight of your spool. If you need more yarn, carefully place it back on the winder and continue.

Step 5: Gently pull on the yarn that crosses the spool at the top (C). This is the yarn end you first attached to the spool. Pull the end out. This will be the end you start with when you begin your project. Tuck it into the side of the cake to secure it.

Step 6: Gently remove the cake from the spool by pulling up and pushing in the spool with your thumbs. Add a tag to note the weight and scrap measurements or use a wider wrap around label with all the details on it.

SCRAP CAKES FOR UNIVERSAL PROJECTS

All the projects in this book have their scrap cake measurements listed. Here are measurements for basic universal projects depending on whether it is worked in increasing rows or rounds or worked flat in equal length rows.

CENTRE START

Centre start projects are worked in increasing rows or rounds.

Scrap cakes 1 and 2 are designed for projects worked in increasing lengths where there are regular increases, for example centre start circles and triangles. You will start with shorter lengths, then, when the rows (or rounds) increase in length, you will increase the yarn lengths.

Depending on which stitch you are using, choose between Scrap cake 1 or 2.

EQUAL ROWS

Scrap cake 3 uses lengths of similar measurement for patterns that are worked in equal rows or rounds throughout using the same stitch.

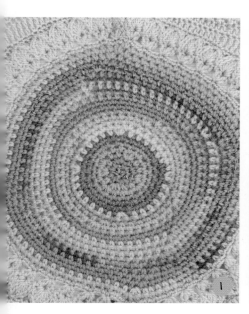

Scrap cake 1

This is suitable for stitches that require less yarn, such as single crochet and half double crochet stitches and patterns that use them, such as moss stitch.

Start with a length of 50cm (20in), then use 10–15 lengths of 50cm (20in). Continue increasing the lengths by 50cm (20in) for each grouping of 10–15 lengths. Increase the lengths in the same amount throughout the scrap cake for consistency, increasing by 50–100cm (20–40in) each group working up to 150cm (60in) then start using arm spans after this: 2 AS then 2.5 AS, then 3 AS etc.

Scrap cake 2

This is suitable for stitches that require more yarn-overs, such as double crochet and treble crochet stitches, and variations of them such as puff- and popcorn stitches.

Start with a length of around 100cm (40in), then use 10–15 lengths of 100cm (40in). Continue increasing the lengths by 100–150cm (40–60in) for each grouping of 10–15 lengths. Increase the lengths in the same amount throughout the scrap cake for consistency, increasing by 100–150cm (40–60in) each group working up to then start using arm spans after 150cm (60in): 2 AS then 3 AS etc.

Scrap cake 3

Scrap cake 3 allows you to build a custom scrap cake for your stitch and row length. Work up the first row and measure the length of yarn needed to reach the point where you want the colour to change. Do not count the yarn needed for the foundation chain/row. A good starting point is using lengths of 1–2AS for projects with small stitches and a row length of around 178–330cm (70–130in), for example a moss stitch blanket. See Getting Started: Example One.

THE PROJECTS

SARAH'S snood

This stylish snood is named after my mother, Sarah, who is my biggest cheerleader. The puff stitch used creates a thick, super warm material that will keep your neck cosy all winter long. The puff stitch is worked in V-shaped clusters that create a visually striking pattern reminiscent of little hearts. Spread the love by making it as a gift!

This is a quick project, using only one scrap cake of 90g (3¼oz) so it is perfect if you are new to making scrap cakes. Once you've made one snood, you won't want to stop – why not make them as presents in all your loved ones' favourite colours.

YOU WILL NEED

YARN

1 x 90g (3¼oz) Scrap cakes
12 x 13.5 AS
2 x 8g (¼oz) of a matching colour
Note: For adjustments in the size work the chainless foundation in a number divisible by 6.
A larger snood will need a larger scrap cake as well as more yarn in the starting/end colour.

HOOKS

o 5mm (H-8)

TOOLS AND NOTIONS

o Measuring tape
o Scissors
o Weighing scales
o Darning needle

MEASUREMENTS

25.5cm (10in) height by 64cm (25in) circumference

TENSION (GAUGE)

5 repeat duo puff sts and 9 rows per 10cm (4in) square

PATTERN

Starting with one of the 8g (¼oz) lengths, make a slip knot, leaving a long yarn tail. Make a chainless foundation of 84 dc.

Round 1: without twisting the chain, join last dc to first dc: drop loop from hook keeping it safe, insert hook in the bottom of the first dc, using the yarn tail, slst into the bottom of the last dc to close.

Round 2: return loop to hook, FP-stsc around the post of the first dc, *BPdc around the next post, FPdc around the next post*; repeat from * to * until the last dc, BPdc into last stitch, slst into the first stsc to close. Cut yarn.

Round 3: join your scrap cake with a slst into the same st, sc into the same st, ch1, sc into the next st, work sc into each st to the end, slst into the first sc to close.

Round 4: *work one ps into the first sc, ch1, work another ps into the same st, skip 2sts*; repeat from * to * to the end, slst into the top of the first ps to close.

Round 5: slst into the first ch1sp. *Work one ps into the ch1sp, ch1, work another ps into the same st*; repeat from * to * to the end, slst into the top of the first ps to close.

Rounds 6–20: repeat Round 5 another 15 times. (17 rows ps)

Round 21: ch1, sc into the same stitch as your slst, *sc into the ch1sp. sc into the top of the next ps twice*; repeat from * to * to the last ps. slst to close. Cut yarn.

Round 22: attach second 8g scrap to the same st as your slst, stsc into the same stitch, dc into each stitch to the end, slst into the stsc to close.

Round 23: repeat Round 2.

Cut your yarn and weave in ends. Block gently to measurements following instructions on ball band.

HESSIAN BAG cover

These square panels can be made for any square hessian tote bag. This project consists of two panels which are sewn onto the main sides of the tote. The tote bag used for this project measures 25.5 x 25.5cm (10 x 10in). There are many sizes of these useful little bags which are great for mini shopping trips or as a gift bag. You can also use them as a crochet project bag.

My crochet panel is stretched to fit a 25.5cm (10in) tote, but you can work up the square to fit your choice of hessian bag. Remember you need to have to stretch the finished square slightly to fit the tote bag or the panels will be too loose.

YOU WILL NEED

YARN

2 x 30g (1oz) Scrap cakes
Make two 30g (1oz) scrap cakes for two 25.5cm (10in) squares
2 x 65cm (25in)
3 x 100cm (40in)
3 x 1 AS
3 x 1 AS + 76cm (30in)
3 x 2 AS + 38cm (15in)
3 x 3 AS + 76cm (30in)
3 x 4 AS + 38cm (15in)
3 x 5 AS
Note: If your bag is bigger, continue to add lengths starting with 3 x 6AS, then 3 x 7AS and so on.

HOOKS
o 4.5mm (7)

TOOLS AND NOTIONS
o Measuring tape
o Scissors
o Weighing scales
o 8 stitch markers
o Strong darning needle

OTHER
o Square hessian tote bag of any size (sample uses 25.5 x 25.5cm/10 x 10in tote)

MEASUREMENTS
25.5 x 25.5cm (10 x 10in) tote bag, or size of your choice

TENSION (GAUGE)
16 sts and 16 rows per 10cm (4in) square

PATTERN

Round 1 (RS): mr, stsc, sc, ch2, *sc, dc, sc, ch2*; repeat from * to * 3 more times, sc into the ring, slst into stsc to close. (12 sts, 4 ch1sp)

Round 2: ch1, sc into st below, *dc in next st, (sc, ch2, sc) into the ch1sp, dc into the next st (maybe hidden under the sc just worked), sc into next st*; repeat from * to * 2 more times, dc into next st, (sc, ch2, sc) into ch1sp, dc into the next st, slst into sc to close.

Round 3: stsc into the st below, sc in next st, dc in next st, (sc, ch2, sc) into the ch1sp, *dc, (sc in next st, dc in next st) up to the next corner, (sc, ch2, sc) into the ch1sp*; repeat from * to * 3 more times, (dc in next st, sc in next st) to start, slst into sc to close.

Round 4: ch1, sc into st below, *dc in next st, (sc in next st, dc in next st up to the next corner, (sc, ch2, sc) into the ch1sp*; repeat from * to * 3 more times, dc in next st, (sc in next st, dc in next st) to start, slst into sc to close.

Repeat Rounds 3 and 4 thirteen more times to fit a 25.5cm (10in) Hessian bag or continue repeating Rows 3 and 4 to fit your size tote bag.

Leave a tail of at least 1 AS + 76cm (30in). This will be used for sewing the piece to the panel. Attach a stitch marker to each corner, and pin the corners to the corners of the tote bag.

Measure your half way point along the sides of the panel and pin to the tote on each side. Start sewing each stitch to the tote. If the tote bag is a particularly tough material, you can catch the threads of the hessian weave to attach your panels instead. I have used a simple running stitch to attach my panels.

Weave in your ends and you have a fancy crochet tote bag. Why not add a cute tassel to the handles?

SUNSHINE
wrap

A fun Boho-style wrap full of colour and with a fabulous centre circle swirl that looks like a wonderful vibrant eye! Or a swirly colourful sun.

For this pattern you will need to make up three scrap cakes, one for the centre circle made up of short to longer lengths; the centre is worked with a simple moss stitch.

The bold choice of colour will require some intermediate skill level but honestly it's very easy and it should be fun to learn new stitches! The left and right 'wing' panels are made with two scrap cakes both with the same measurements.

YOU WILL NEED

YARN

Yarn 1: 30–35g (1–1¼oz) Scrap cake
1 x 50cm (20in)
2 x 100cm (40in)
1 x 1 AS
1 x 2 AS
20 x 1–3 AS
Yarn 2: 100g (3½oz) of one shade
Yarns 3 and 4: 185g (6½oz) Scrap cakes
Use the same measurements for each and 20/25 different colours
50 x 6½ AS
Extra scraps for border and tassels or pompoms as desired

HOOKS
o 4mm (G-6)

TOOLS AND NOTIONS
o Stitch marker
o Weighing scales
o Darning needles

MEASUREMENTS
Full shawl from corner to corner: 190cm (74.5in)

Central 'Eye': 25.5cm (10in) across

TENSION (GAUGE)
Per 10cm (4in): 21 rows and 11 repeats per row

PATTERN

SUNSHINE SPIRAL

Use Yarn 1 to begin the moss st spiral. Note where the increase is placed in each round; it sits into the first st of the previous round.

Round 1 (RS): mr, (1sc, ch1) 4 times into the ring. Do not join and work in an ongoing spiral. (4 sc, (4 ch1sp)

Round 2: (2sc, ch1) into first ch1sp, (1sc, ch1) 2 times into each subsequent ch1sp. (8 sc, 8 ch1sp)

Round 3: *(2sc, ch1) into next ch1sp, (1sc, ch1) into next ch1sp*; repeat from * to * 4 times. (12 sc, 8 ch1sp)

Round 4: *(2sc, ch1) into next ch1sp, (1sc, ch1) into next 2 ch1sp*; repeat from * to * 4 times. (16 sc, 12 ch1sp)

Round 5: *(2sc, ch1) into next ch1sp, (1sc, ch1) into next 3 ch1sp*; repeat from * to * 4 times. (20 sc, 16 ch1sp)

Round 6: *(2sc, ch1) into next ch1sp, (1sc, ch1) into next 4 ch1sp*; repeat from * to * 4 times. (24 sc, 20 ch1sp)

Round 7: *(2sc, ch1) into next ch1sp, (1sc, ch1) into next 5 ch1sp*; repeat from * to * 4 times. (28 sc, 24 ch1sp)

Round 8: *(2sc, ch1) into next ch1sp, (1sc, ch1) into next 6 ch1sp*; repeat from * to * 4 times. (32 sc, 28 ch1sp)

Round 9: *(2sc, ch1) into next ch1sp, (1sc, ch1) into next 7 ch1sp*; repeat from * to * 4 times. (36 sc, 32 ch1sp)

Round 10: *(2sc, ch1) into next ch1sp, (1sc, ch1) into next 8 ch1sp*; repeat from * to * 4 times. (40 sc, 36 ch1sp)

Round 11: *(2sc, ch1) into next ch1sp, (1sc, ch1) into next 9 ch1sp*; repeat from * to * 4 times. (44 sc, 40 ch1sp)

Round 12: *(2sc, ch1) into next ch1sp, (1sc, ch1) into next 10 ch1sp*; repeat from * to * 4 times. (48 sc, 44 ch1sp)

Round 13: *(2sc, ch1) into next ch1sp, (1sc, ch1) into next 11 ch1sp*; repeat from * to * 4 times. (52 sc, 48 ch1sp)

Round 14: *(2sc, ch1) into next ch1sp, (1sc, ch1) into next 12 ch1sp*; repeat from * to * 4 times. (56 sc, 52 ch1sp)

Round 15: *(2sc, ch1) into next ch1sp, (1sc, ch1) into next 13 ch1sp*; repeat from * to * 4 times. (60 sc, 56 ch1sp)

Round 16: *(2sc, ch1) into next ch1sp, (1sc, ch1) into next 14 ch1sp*; repeat from * to * 4 times. (64 sc, 60 ch1sp)

Round 17: *(2sc, ch1) into next ch1sp, (1sc, ch1) into next 15 ch1sp*; repeat from * to * 4 times. (68 sc, 64 ch1sp)

Round 18: *(2sc, ch1) into next ch1sp, (1sc, ch1)1 into next 16 ch1sp*; repeat from * to * 4 times. (72 sc, 68 ch1sp)

Round 19: *(2sc, ch1) into next ch1sp, (1sc, ch1) into next 17 ch1sp*; repeat from * to * 4 times. (76 sc, 72 ch1sp)

Round 20: *(2sc, ch1) into next ch1sp, (1sc, ch1) into next 18 ch1sp*; repeat from * to * 4 times. (80 sc, 76 ch1sp)

Round 21: *(2sc, ch1) into next ch1sp, (1sc, ch1) into next 19 ch1sp*; repeat from * to * 4 times. (84 sc, 80 ch1sp)

Round 22: *(2sc, ch1) into next ch1sp, (1sc, ch1) into next 20 ch1sp*; repeat from * to * 4 times. (88 sc, 84 ch1sp)

Round 23: *(2sc, ch1) into next ch1sp, (1sc, ch1) into next 21 ch1sp*; repeat from * to * 4 times. (92 sc, 88 ch1sp)

Round 24: *(2sc, ch1) into next ch1sp, (1sc, ch1) into next 22 ch1sp*; repeat from * to * 4 times. (96 sc, 92 ch1sp)

Final sc should be situated into ch1sp in between next 2 sc. Secure st safely for further working. Gently block to measurements.

SQUARE

Join Yarn 2 to any chsp.

Round 25: (1sc, ch1) into next ch1sp (place marker in this st), (1sc, ch1) into next ch1sp*; repeat from * to * to marker placed in this round. (96 sc, 92 ch1sp)

Begin working in joined rounds.

Round 26: 1stdc into next st, remove stitch marker, (1dc, ch1, 2dc) in same ch1sp, *skip 2 ch1sp, (2dc, ch1, 2dc) in next ch1sp, skip 2 ch1sp*; repeat from * to * end, slst into top of stdc to close. (34 groups of repeats, 136 dc)

Round 27: *4dc into next ch1sp, ch1, 4dc in same space, slst after second dc and before 3rd dc*; repeat from * to * end, slst into slst from Round 26 to close. (272 sts, 34 ch1sp)

Round 28 (WS): turn to work into back of petals, ch1, 1sc into slst from Round 27, *ch4, skip 8 dc, 1sc into 2 bars from slst in Round 27 (looks like a V, between last and first dc of each petal)*; repeat from * to * to end, slst into first sc to close, turn. (34 ch4sp, 34 sts)

Round 29 (RS): slst into next ch4sp, stdc, 4dc into same chsp, (5dc into next ch4sp) 33 times, slst into first dc to close. (170 sts)

Round 30: 1sc into next 2 sts, 1sc into ch1sp between sets of 4dc in Round 27, skip 1 st, 1sc into next 2 sts, *1sc into next 2 sts, 1sc into ch1sp between sets of 4dc in Round 27, skip 1 st, 1sc into next 2 sts*; repeat from * to * end, slst into first sc to close. (170 sts)

Place stitch maker in sts 22, 64, 106 and 148 to mark corners, and move up to middle of corner on each round.

Round 31: ch1, 1sc into next 6 sts, 1hdc into next 7 sts, 1dc into next 7 sts, 1tr into next st, (2tr, ch2, 2tr) into next st (corner), *1tr into next st, 1dc into next 7 sts, 1hdc into next 7 sts, 1sc into next 11 sts, 1hdc into next 7 sts, 1dc in next 7 sts, 1tr into next st, (2tr, ch2, 2tr) into next st (corner)*; repeat from * to * 2 more times, 1tr into next st, 1dc into next 7 sts, 1hdc into next 7 sts, 1sc into next 5 sts, slst into top of sc to close. (180 sts)

Round 32: ch1, 1sc into next 9 sts, 1hdc into next 4 sts, 1dc into next 2 sts, 1tr into next 8 sts, (3tr, ch2, 3tr) into next ch2sp (corner), *1tr into next 8 sts, 1dc into next 2 sts, 1dc into next 4 sts, 1sc into next 17 sts, 1hdc into next 4 sts, 1dc into next 2 sts, 1tr into next 8 sts, (3tr, ch2, 3tr) into next ch2sp (corner)*; repeat from * to * 2 times more, 1 tr into next 8 sts, 1dc into next 2 sts, 1hdc into next 4 sts, 1sc into next 8 sts, slst into top of sc. (204 sts)

Round 33: ch1, 1sc into next 8 sts, 1hdc into next 10 sts, 1dc into next 4 sts, 1tr into next 3 sts, 5tr into ch2sp (place marker into 3rd tr), *1tr into next 3 sts, 1dc into next 4 sts, 1hdc into next 10 sts, 1sc into next 16 sts, 1hdc into next 10 sts, 1dc into next 4 sts, 1tr into next 3 sts, 5tr into ch2sp (place marker into 3rd tr),*; repeat from * to * 2 more times, 1tr into next 3 sts, 1dc into next 4 sts, 1hdc into next 10 sts, 1sc into remaining 8 sts, slst into sc to close. (224 sts)

Round 34: ch1, 1sc into same stitch as ch1, **1tr into next st, 1sc into next st*; repeat from ** to * to marker, (1sc, ch1, 1sc) into marked st (corner), 1sc into next st, 1tr into next st**; repeat from ** to ** 3 times, slst into first sc to close. (226 sts)

Round 35: slst into next st, stdc into same st as slst from Round 34, **ch1, 1dc into next st, ch1*; repeat from ** to * to ch1sp corner, (1dc, ch2, 1dc) into ch1sp; repeat from ** to * 3 more times, slst into first dc to close. (230 sts)

Round 36: ch1, **2sc into next ch1sp, skip 1 st*; repeat from ** to * to ch2sp corner, (2sc, ch1, 2sc) into ch2sp; repeat from ** to * 3 more times. (242 sts)

Round 37: ch1, 1sc into same st as slst, **ch1, skip 1 st, 1sc into next st*; repeat from ** to * to the ch1sp corner, (1sc, ch2, 1sc) in ch1sp*; repeat from ** to * 3 more times. (148 sts, 148 chsp)

Break Yarn 2 and weave in ends. Join Yarn 3 in any corner.

SIDE PANELS

Row 1: 1sc into ch2sp, *ch1, 1sc into next ch1sp*; repeat from * to * to next ch2sp (corner), (1sc, ch2, 1sc) into ch2sp, **ch1, 1sc into next ch1sp**; repeat from ** to ** to next ch2sp corner, 1sc into ch2sp, turn.

Row 2: ch1, 1sc into next ch1sp, *ch1, 1sc into next ch1sp*; repeat from * to * to ch2sp (corner), (1sc, ch, 1sc) into ch2sp; **ch1, 1sc into next ch1sp**; repeat from ** to ** to last ch1sp, 1sc into last st, turn.

Repeat Row 2 until Yarn 3 is finished.

Join Yarn 4 at opposite corner to Yarn 3 join. Repeat Row 1 and then work Row 2 until Yarn 4 is nearly finished, finishing at end of a row.

With your pile of any scraps ready to join as you go, work last of remaining yarn from Yarns 3 and 4 down the sides of the rows, working 1sc into each row end around the entire wrap. When I reached the corners of the square I worked sc2tog to help with any rippling that might occur. Joining new yarns as you feel you need to switch colours, this part is all yours! Use your creative brain to figure out what works best on your scarf.

On the two end points of the wrap you can attach a matching tassel or a pompom, whichever you fancy! I have found that giving the wrap a good stretch and pull to straighten all the stitches can shape it perfectly but if you prefer to block the sides then this will help, too.

TULIP
tote bag

This tote bag is a fun accessory that is big enough to hold all your essentials and has two handy strap sizes so you can wear it as a shoulder or cross-body bag. Made holding two yarns together – the scrap cake with another coordinating solid colour – this is a colourful make.

Crocheted in the round from the base of the bag up, this is a fun project that works up quickly. The combination of increases and slip stitches makes an eye-catching, wavy design which is a great a way to use up your scraps.

YOU WILL NEED

YARN

1 x 100g (3½oz) Scrap cake
Each scrap cake will require the following lengths:
1 x 117cm (46in)
1 x 168cm (66in)
1 x 1 AS + 76cm (30in)
3 x 2 AS
3 x 3 AS
3 x 4 AS
19 x 5 AS
100g (3½oz) ball of a solid shade

HOOKS

o 5mm (H-8)

TOOLS AND NOTIONS

o Measuring tape
o Scissors
o Weighing scales
o 4 stitch markers
o Darning needle

MEASUREMENTS

Bag: 38cm (15in) height and 35.5cm (14in) width

Long strap: 84cm (33in) length

Short strap: 34.5cm (13½in) length

TENSION (GAUGE)

15 sts and 7 rows per 10cm (4in) square

PATTERN

Use scrap cake held together with contrast shade.

Round 1 (RS): mr, stsc, 2dc into the ring, ch2, *3dc, ch2*; repeat from * to * 2 more times, slst into the stsc to close. (12sts, 4 ch1sp)

Round 2: stsc into the first st/slst, 1dc into each st up to corner, *(2dc, ch2, 2dc) into the ch1sp, 1dc each st up to corner*; repeat from * to * 2 more times, (2dc, ch2, 2dc) into ch1sp, 2dc into each st to end.

Rounds 3–7: Repeat Round 2. (108 sts, 4 ch1sp)

Place a st marker into the 12th st on each side. Replace this marker into the 12th st each round.

For the start of each round we will need to TURN and slst back two sts to the 12th st from the RS corner.

Round 8 (RS): skipping 3sts, dc2tog (12th and 16th st), *1dc in each st to the next corner, (2dc, ch2, 2dc) into the ch1sp, 1dc into next 11sts, dc2tog skipping 3sts and joining 12th and 16th sts*; repeat from * to * 2 more times, 1dc into next 11sts.

Rounds 9–17: Repeat Round 8 a further 8 times, remembering to TURN and slst back two sts before commencing each round.

Cut yarn.

STRAP & HANDLE (MAKE 2)

This design has two strap options: one as a handle and the other as a shoulder strap. You can make both short or both long, depending on what you fancy!

Starting ch2 counts as first st throughout.

Leave along tail for sewing, ch12.

Row 1 (RS): 1dc into the 3rd ch from the hook, 1dc into each st to the end. (11 sts)

Row 2 (WS): ch2, *FPdc next st, BPdc next st*; repeat from * to * to the end. (11 sts)

For the longer strap (79cm/31in):

Rows 3–53: repeat Row 2 another 50 times (or to however long your straps should be to fit your needs)

For the handle (28cm/11in):

Rows 3–20: repeat Row 2 another 17 times (or to however long your straps should be to fit your needs)

Cut yarn leaving a long tail (to sew the strap or handle to the body of the bag.)

Thread the long tail onto a darning needle. Attach each end of the strap to a corner point on the main body of the bag. Lay the first two rows of the strap to the back of the point and sew across.

Attach the opposite end of the strap to the opposite corner point of the bag and repeat sewing.

Repeat for the handle or second strap.

A

B

TRIANGLE PUFF shawl

A colourful triangle makes up the centre of this shawl, framed by two wings in a solid shade of your choice. Keep warm on cool summer evenings or keep cosy in the midst of winter – this shawl will be the highlight of any outfit.

The shawl is made using the puff stitch, which creates a thick fabric that works up quickly. Use any colours you like for the triangle and frame it with a neutral, or go crazy and add another bold colour!

YOU WILL NEED

YARN

1 x 170g (6oz) Scrap cake
Use Scrap Cake 2 measurements from Scrap Cakes for Universal Projects.
Tip: You can split your scrap cake into two smaller cakes for ease of winding, Just remember to label them so you start with the right one!
2 x 100g (3½oz) ball of any matching shade

HOOKS
o 5mm (H-8)

TOOLS AND NOTIONS
o Measuring tape
o Scissors
o Weighing scales
o Stitch marker
o Darning needle

MEASUREMENTS
50cm (20in) height and 181.5cm (71½in) width

TENSION (GAUGE)
8 puff sts (7 ch1sp) and 10 rows per 10cm (4in) square

PATTERN

TRIANGLE
Use scrap cake for triangle.

Row 1 (RS): mr, stsc into the mr, (ch1, ps into the mr) three times, ch2, (ps into the mr, ch1) three times, 1dc into mr, turn. (1 stsc, 6 ps, 6 ch1sp, 1 ch2sp, 1 dc)

Row 2: stsc into the first st, *ch1, ps into the next ch1sp*; repeat from * to * 2 more times, (ch1, ps) 3 times into the ch2sp, **ch1, ps into the next ch1sp **; repeat from ** to ** two more times, ch1, 1dc into the last st, turn. (1 stsc, 9 ps, 10 ch1sp, 1 dc)

Row 3: stsc into the first st, (ch1, ps) into each of the next 5 ch1sp, ch1, (ps, ch1, ps) into the top of the next ps, place a marker into the central ch1sp just made, (ch1, ps) into each of the next 5 ch1sp, ch1, dc into the top of the stsc below, turn. (1 stsc, 12 ps, 13 ch1sp, 1 dc)

Row 4: stsc into the first st, (ch1, ps) into each ch1sp to marked ch1sp, (ch1, ps) 3 times into marked ch1sp, remove marker and place a marker into the central ps, (ch1, ps) into each remaining ch1sp, ch1, dc into the top of the stsc below, turn. (3 ps increased)

Row 5: stsc into the first st, (ch1, ps) into each ch1sp up to marked ps, ch1, (ps, ch1, ps) into top of marked st, remove marker and place marker into central ch1sp just made, (ch1, ps) into each remaining ch1sp, ch1, dc into the top of the stsc below, turn. (3 ps increased)

Rows 6–63: repeat Rows 4–5.

Row 34: repeat Row 4. (105 ps)

SIDES

Join your contrast shade to the beginning of the RS. Attach with a slst to the top of the stsc.

Row 1 (RS): stsc into the same st as the slst, *ch1, cl into the next ch1sp*; repeat from * to * to ch1sp BEFORE the corner ch2sp, ch1, 1sc into the last ch1sp, slst into the corner ch2sp, turn.

Row 2 (WS): slst into the next st, ch2, skip one ch1sp, *cl into next ch1sp, ch1*; repeat from * to * for all ch1sp, ch1, 1dc into stsc, turn.

Row 3 (RS): stsc into first st, *ch1, cl into the next ch1sp*; repeat from * to * until one ch1sp and ch2sp remain, ch1, 1sc into ch1sp, slst into ch2sp, turn.

Rows 3–34: repeat Rows 2 and 3, ending with a Row 2 (WS).

Cut yarn.

Repeat for the second side.

FINISHING

Weave in ends and block to desired measurements. You can finish your shawl with a set of scrappy tassels or pompoms if you want.

DAVE'S
blanket

Named after my late father, Dave, this
cosy and heavy blanket will feel like an
extra warm hug. It is made using two
yarns held together, which gives it extra
warmth, but it has the added advantage
of being a quick and easy make.

Pick your three favourite colour themes
for each of the three block sections or
use the same for the outside sections
with a contrast accent in the middle.
Personally, I love mustards and turquoise,
so I paired them with a grey shade to have
three distinct sections that complement
each other.

YOU WILL NEED

YARN

4 x 110g (4oz) Scrap cakes
Each scrap cake will require the following lengths:
7–11 AS until desired weight
Note: Tie them in any random order. Consider which colour you will choose for Yarn 2 and avoid colours that are too similar.
5 x 100g (3½oz) skeins (hanks) of one or more solid colours
Note: 440g (15½oz) required of your chosen colour for the 2nd yarn. (I chose three colours: Peacock Blue x 2, Grey x 2, and Mustard x 1)

HOOKS
o   6mm (J-10)

TOOLS AND NOTIONS
o   Measuring tape
o   Scissors
o   Weighing scales
o   Darning needle

MEASUREMENTS
106.5 x 137cm (42 x 54in)

TENSION (GAUGE)
11 sts and 6 rows per 10cm (4in) square

PATTERN

Holding a scrap cake and one of the solid colours together, make a chainless foundation of 90 dc.

Row 1 (RS): ch1, sc into each st to the end, turn. (90 sc)

Row 2 (WS): ch1, dc into each st to the end, turn. (90 dc)

Rows 3–94: repeat Rows 1 and 2.

Row 95 (RS): repeat Row 1.

Cut yarn and weave in ends.

Now you can add a fringe or tassels in each corner. Alternatively, you can leave it as a straight edge, as they say – less is more!

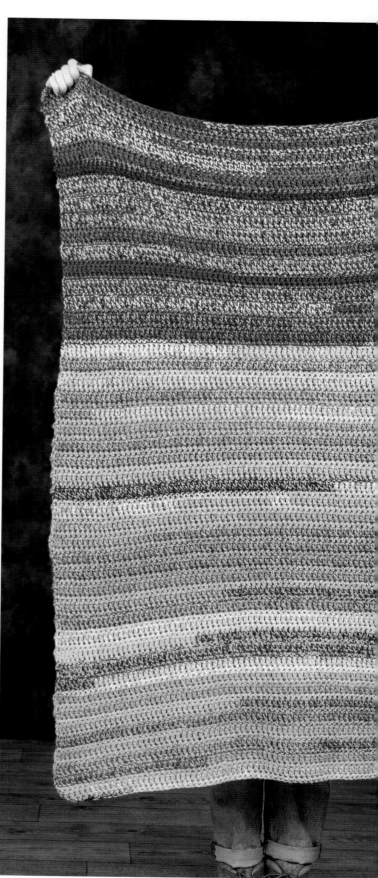

CORNER TO CORNER blanket

Corner to corner blankets are a classic for a reason. It is a lot of fun to see your work expand each row on the first half. Then, the second half feels like a breeze as each row gets shorter and goes quicker!

You'll need two scrap cakes for this blanket, made the exact opposite from each other, to match the two halves of the blanket – one growing in size, one shrinking.

YOU WILL NEED

YARN

Yarn 1: 200g (7oz) Scrap cake
1 x 112cm (44in)
1 x 1 AS + 10cm (4in)
1 x 1 AS + 84cm (33in)
2 x 2 AS
2 x 2 AS + 66cm (26in)
3 x 3 AS + 50cm (20in)
4 x 5 AS
5 x 7 AS
7 x 9 AS
8 x 11 AS (7g/¼oz each)
8 x 13 AS (9g/3/8oz each)
Yarn 2: 200g (7oz) Scrap cake
Note: Use the same measurements as for Scrap cake 1, but starting with the longest length. Each cake should weigh around 200g (7oz).
Yarn 3: 400g (14oz) ball of a contrast shade
Note: 4 x 100g (3½oz) of your chosen single shade for the accent shade. A neutral will work best with any vibrant colourway or a strong colour to contrast a more neutral scrap cake colourway. I used the beach pebbles colourway for my scrap cake and chose a light grey as the contrast shade.

HOOKS

o 6mm (J-10)

TOOLS AND NOTIONS

o Measuring tape
o Scissors
o Weighing scales
o Darning needle

MEASUREMENTS

119.5 x 119.5cm (47 x 47in)

TENSION (GAUGE)

4 rows by 4 rows per 10cm (4in) square

PATTERN

INCREASE SIDE

Holding Yarn 1 and Yarn 3 together, make a slip knot on your hook and ch6.

Row 1 (RS): ch6, dc into 4th ch from the hook, dc into the next 2 ch, turn. (3 dc, 3 ch).

Row 2 (WS): dc into 4th ch from hook, dc into the next 2 ch, slst under the ch3sp from Row 1 to join, ch3, 3dc into the same ch3sp, turn. (6 dc, 2 ch3sp)

Row 3: ch6, 1dc into 4th ch from the hook, dc into the next 2 ch, slst under the ch3sp, *ch3, 3dc into the same ch3sp, slst under the next ch3sp*; repeat from * to * to last ch3sp, ch3, 3dc into the same ch3sp, turn. (9 dc, 3 ch3sp)

Rows 4–48: Repeat Row 3.

DECREASE SIDE

Switch to using Yarn 2 and Yarn 3 held together.

Row 49: slst into the next 3dc and ch3sp, *ch3, 3dc into the same ch-3-sp, slst under next ch3sp*; repeat from * to * to the last ch3sp on the row, slst into the ch3sp, turn.

Rows 50–94: repeat Row 49.

On last row, cut yarn and pull through slst. Weave in ends and block to measurements.

You can add a fringe to the edge or tassels to the corners as you prefer.

PISA
cowl

Fun and textured, this cowl has a beautiful drape and can provide a unique accent piece to any outfit.

It is a quick make and even the 130g (4½oz) scrap cake will be quick to build. The interlocking stitches create an extra layer of interplay between your chosen colours in a fun, random way that adds to the scrappy nature of the project. For a dramatic look, choose colours with lots of contrast.

YOU WILL NEED

YARN

1 x 130g (4½oz) Scrap cake
Use lengths between ½ AS and 2 AS, randomly joined until 130g is reached.

HOOKS

o 5mm (H-8)

TOOLS AND NOTIONS

o Measuring tape
o Scissors
o Weighing scales
o Darning needle

MEASUREMENTS

43 x 33cm (17 x 13in)

TENSION (GAUGE)

14 sts and 7 rows (a double layered row counts as one) per 10cm (4in) square

PATTERN

Make a chainless foundation of 120 hdc.

Round 1 (RS): making sure not to twist the chain, join the last st to the first st with slst into the bottom of the first ch and the top of the first st to close.

Round 2: sttr into the first st, *ch1, skip 1 st, 1tr into the next st*; repeat from * to * to one st from the end of the round, ch1 and slst into the top of the first tr to close the round. (60 tr, 60 ch1sp)

Round 3: ch1, 1sc into the first st, *1tr into the skipped st the row below, 1sc into the next st*; repeat fr * to * to the last st, 1tr into the last skipped st below, slst into the first sc to close the round. (60 tr, 60 sc)

Round 4: ch1, 1hdc into the first st, hdc into each st around, slst into the last st to close the round. (120 hdc)

Rounds 5–31: repeat Rounds 2–4 another 9 times.

Cut yarn and weave in ends. Block to measurements.

Embrace the colour combinations as they happen, but if you really don't like it or the colours seem too similar, you can always cut your yarn and add an extra length in a different colour.

GRANNY
square
blanket

This classic granny square blanket is a fun, relaxing make. Choose colours to make it a retro hit or use a modern palette to update the look – the granny square blanket is nothing if not versatile.

Starting with a large 200g (7oz) scrap cake, it can be extended continuously as long as you have more scraps to add to it. Just keep going until you are happy with the size.

YOU WILL NEED

YARN

1 x 200g (7oz) or more Scrap cake
Use Scrap Cake 2 measurements from Scrap Cakes for Universal Projects.

HOOKS

o 4mm (G-6)

TOOLS AND NOTIONS

o Measuring tape
o Scissors
o Weighing scales
o Darning needle

MEASUREMENTS

Variable, depending on amount of yarn used

TENSION (GAUGE)

5 trios and 7 rows per 10cm (4in) square

SPECIAL ABBREVIATION

TRIO: 3dc same space (granny stitch)

PATTERN

Round 1: mr, stsc into the ring, 2dc into the ring, ch2, *3dc into the ring, ch2*; repeat from *to* 2 more times, slst into the top of the stsc to close, turn.

Round 2: stsc into ch2sp, 2dc into the (ch2sp, ch2, 3dc) into the same ch2sp, *(3dc, ch2, 3dc) into the next ch2sp*; repeat from * to * 2 more times, slst into the top of the stsc, turn.

Round 3: stsc into the space below (between the sets of 3dc), 2dc into the same space, *(3dc, ch2, 3dc) into the next ch2sp, 3dc into the space between the trios*; repeat from * to * 2 more times, (3dc, ch2, 3dc) into ch2sp, slst into the top of the stsc to close, turn.

Round 4: stsc into the space below, 2dc into the same space, *(3dc, ch2, 3dc) into ch2sp, 3dc into each space between the trios to next corner*; repeat from * to * another 2 times, (3dc, ch2, 3dc) into ch2sp, 3dc into each space between the trios to beginning, slst into the top of the stsc to close, turn.

Round 5: stsc into the space below, 2dc into the same space, *3dc into each space between the trios to corner, (3dc, ch2, 3dc) into ch2sp*; repeat from * to * another 3 times, 3dc into each space between the trios to start, slst into the top of the stsc to close, turn.

Repeat Round 5, turning after every round, until your desired size (or you run out of yarn!).

Cut yarn and weave in ends. Block to measurements. Add a fringe or tassels for extra fun!

POT
cover

Pots are great vessels for storing all sorts
of things, from dressing table clutter to
pot plants. This project is a great way to
brighten up your interior and upcycle at
the same time.

The covers are crocheted in the round
from the centre bottom and the width
and height can be adapted depended on
what size pot you have. They are a quick
and easy make and the perfect way to
brighten up a room or windowsill.

YOU WILL NEED

YARN

1 x 60–70g (21/8–2½oz) Scrap cake
½–1 AS lengths until desired weight in random order.

HOOKS

o 4mm (G-6)

TOOLS AND NOTIONS

o Measuring tape
o Scissors
o Weighing scales
o 4 stitch markers
o Darning needle

OTHER

o Pot with a 15cm (6in) base

MEASUREMENTS

Variable, depending on your pot

TENSION (GAUGE)

17 sts and 12 rows per 10cm (4in) square over alternating dc and sc rows

SPECIAL ABBREVIATIONS

hdc-slst: yo, insert hook into the stitch indicated, yo and pull through all loops on hook.

Side post sc: Looking at the dc stitch from the WS the st has a bar to the right, use this bar to work your sc into.

PATTERN

Ch1 at the beginning of the row does not count as a stitch.

BASE

Round 1 (RS): mr, 12dc into the ring, slst into the first st to close. (12 dc)

Round 2: ch1, 2sc into the next st, 2sc into each of the next 11 sts, slst into the first st to close. (24 sc)

Round 3: stsc into the first st, *2dc into the next st, 1dc into the next st*; repeat from * to * to last st remaining, 2dc into the last st, slst into the first st to close. (36 dc)

Round 4: ch1, *1sc into the next 2 sts, 2sc into the next st*; repeat from * to * to end, slst into the first st to close. (48 sc)

Round 5: stsc into the first st, 1dc into the next 2 sts, *2dc into the next st placing marker into the second st, 1dc into the next sts*; repeat from * to * to the last st, 2dc into last st placing marker into the second st, slst into the first st to close. (60 sts – 11.5cm/4½in diameter)

Round 6: ch1, *1sc into the each st to marked st, 2sc into the marked st moving marker up to second st*; repeat from * to * to end, slst into the first st to close. (72 sc)

Round 7: stsc into the first st, 1dc into each st to marked st, *2dc into the next st moving marker up to second st, 1dc each st to marked st*; repeat to the last st remaining, 2dc into last st moving marker up to next st, slst into the first st to close. (84 sc)

For a pot with a 15cm (6in) base, stop here. If your pot is larger, repeat Rounds 6 and 7 as needed. Your base will seem smaller than your pot but remember it will need to fit snugly to avoid slipping. Block your base if desired.

SIDE

Row 1 (RS): ch1, 1sc into each st to THIRD marker, sc2tog, 1sc into each st to the SIXTH marker, sc2tog, 1sc into each st to the NINTH marker, sc2tog, 1sc into each st to the last marker, sc2tog, slst to close, turn. (78sts for the 15cm/6in base, decreased by 4 sts).

Row 2 (WS): stsc into first st, dc to end of round, slst to close, turn.

Row 3: sc to end of round, slst to close, turn.

Rows 4–23: repeat Row 2 and Row 3 ten more times for a post 18cm (7in) tall.

For different pots, repeat as often as needed.

Row 24 (WS): (hdc-slst, ch1) into each st, slst into the first hdc-slst to close the round, turn.

Row 25 (RS): ch1, (sc into the bar of the dc 3 rows down) for each st around, slst into the first sc to close.

Cut yarn.

Your pot is ready to be covered. The final rows are part of the edge lip to help hold it up and the hdc-slst should be protruding from the sides.

CLUTCH
purse

This cute clutch- style purse is made using a combination of different stitches including puff stitch and interlocking crochet, making it a fun project to try.

The purse is constructed by crocheting in rows with the decorative stitches forming a semi circle at one end. The sides are joined up to form the body of the bag and the half circle folds over to form the closure at the front of the bag.

YOU WILL NEED

YARN

1 x 50g (1¾oz) Scrap cake
½–1 AS lengths until desired weight in random order.

HOOKS

o 5mm (H-8)

TOOLS AND NOTIONS

o Measuring tape
o Scissors
o Weighing scales
o Darning needle

MEASUREMENTS

12.5cm (5in) height and 25.5cm (10in) width when top flap closed

TENSION (GAUGE)

16 sts and 12 rows per 10cm (4in) square over body pattern

PATTERN

Make a chainless foundation of 41 hdc.

Row 1 (RS): work 3 more hdc into the last chain, turn to work 1hdc into the chain on the reverse side of the chainless foundation, ch1, turn. (84 hdc)

Row 2: 1sc into the next 40 sts, 2sc into each of the next 4 sts, 1sc into the next 40 sts, ch1, turn. (88 sts)

Row 3: 1sc into the next 40 sts, *2sc into the next st, 1sc into the next st*; repeat from * to * 3 more times, 1sc into the next 40 sts, ch3, turn. (92 sts)

Row 4: 1dc into the next 40 sts, (cl, ch1) into the next 12 sts, 1dc into the next 40 sts, turn. (92 sts and 12 ch1sp)

Row 5: ch1, 1sc into the next 40 sts, *1sc into the ch1sp, FPsc around the cluster st*; repeat from * to * 11 more times, 1sc into the next 40 sts, turn. (104 sts)

Row 6: ch3, 1dc into the next 40 sts, *(ps, ch1, ps) into the next st, skip 1 st*; repeat from * to * over the next 22 sts, 1dc into the next 40 sts, turn. (104 sts, 12 ch1sp)

Row 7: ch1, 1sc into the next 40 sts, *yo, insert hook around top of next ps and pull up a loop (A), yo two times (B) and insert hook between the two ps and into the same st the ps sits in Row 5 (C), yo and pull through two loops (D), yo and pull through two loops again (E), yo, insert hook into top of next ps and pull up a loop (F), yo and pull through all four loops, ch1 (G)*; repeat from * to * to last ps, 1sc into the next 40 sts.

Row 8: ch1, 1dc into the next 40 sts, 3dc into each of the 12 ch1sp, 1dc into each st to end, turn. (116 sts)

Row 9: ch1, 1sc into the next 40 sts, *2sc into the next st, 1sc into the next 10 sts*; repeat from * to * 2 more times, 2sc into the next st, 1sc into the next 42 sts, turn. (120 sts)

Row 10: ch 3, 1dc into the next 40 sts, *2dc into the next st, 1dc into the next 10 sts*; repeat from * to * 2 more times, 2dc into the next st, 1dc into the next 46 sts, turn. (124 sts)

Row 11: ch1, 1sc into next 41 sts, *FPtr around middle dc from trio set of Row 8, 1sc into next 4 sts*; repeat from * to * 9 more times, FPtr around middle dc from next trio on Row 8, 1sc into next 2 sts, FPtr around middle dc from last trio set on Row 8, 1sc into next 41 sts. (136 sts, 12 FPtr)

Row 12: ch3, 1dc into each st to the end, turn. (136 sts)

Row 13: ch1, 1sc into the next 40 sts, *1sc, ch2*; repeat from * to * for the next 56 sts, 1sc into the next 40 sts, turn. (136 sts and 56 ch1sp)

Row 14: ch1, 1hdc into the next 40 sts, FPhdc around each of the next 56 sc, skipping the ch2, 1hdc into the next 40 sts, turn. (136 sts)

Row 15: ch1, 1dc into the next 40 sts, *2dc into the next st, 1dc into the next 10 sts*; repeat from * to * 4 more times, 2dc into the next st, 1dc into the next 40 sts, turn. (142 sts)

Row 16: ch1, 1sc into each st to the end, turn. (142 sts)

Row 17: ch1, 1sc into the next 40 sts, *(ch2, slst) into the next st*; repeat from * to * for 62 sts, 1sc into the next 40 sts. (142 sts).

Cut your yarn leaving a long tail. With WS facing, fold up the straight edge to bring it to the 40th st marked either side. Sew down edges using a blanket st. Sew in the tail. Repeat with scrap yarn to sew up the opposite side. Fold your round opening down to close your purse! Block to desired measurements.

BALLOON
pillow

This fun, textured pillow will brighten up your living room. The unique and wonderful design looks fabulous worked up with a scrap cake. The use of front and back post double crochet stitches allows the colours to interplay in a fun and unique way.

The balloon stitch is a great stitch to learn and requires little effort. It covers one side, while a double crochet stitch makes the back easy to work up in a contrast colour. Choose a neutral to match your decor, or go wild with another bright colour.

YOU WILL NEED

YARN

1 x 150g (5¼oz) Scrap cake
2–3 AS lengths until desired weight in random order.
100g (3½oz) ball of a solid contrast shade for back

HOOKS

o 4mm (G-6)

TOOLS AND NOTIONS

o Measuring tape
o Scissors
o Weighing scales
o Darning needle

OTHER

o 43cm (17in) square pillow insert

MEASUREMENTS

43cm (17in) height and width when stretched over pillow

TENSION (GAUGE)

19 sts and 9 rows per 10cm (4in) square balloon st

16 sts and 8 rows per 10cm (4in) square over dc

PATTERN

FRONT

Starting ch3 counts as st throughout.

Make a slip knot on your hook and ch77.

Row 1 (RS): ch77, 4dc into the 4th chain from the hook. *1dc into the next 2 ch, dc7tog over the next 7 ch, 1dc into the next 2 ch, (7dc) into the next ch*; repeat from * to * 4 more times, 1dc into the next 2ch, dc7tog over next 7 ch, 1dc into the next 2 ch, 4dc into the next ch, 1dc into the last ch, turn. (75 sts)

Row 2 (WS): ch3, 1BPdc around the next 4 sts, *1FPdc around the next 2 sts, 1BPdc around the next st, 1FPdc around the next 2 sts, 1BPdc around the next 7 sts*; repeat from * to * 4 more times, 1FPdc around the next 2 sts, 1BPdc around the next st, 1FPdc around the next 2 sts, 1BPdc around the next 4 sts, 1dc into the 3rd starting ch, turn.

Row 3 (RS): ch3, FPdc around the next 4 sts, *1BPdc around the next 2 sts, 1FPdc around the next st, 1BPdc around the next 2 sts, 1FPdc around the next 7 sts*; repeat from * to * 4 more times, 1BPdc around the next 2 sts, 1FPdc around the next st, 1BPdc around the next 2 sts, 1FPdc around the next 4 sts, 1dc into the 3rd ch, turn.

Row 4 (WS): repeat Row 2.

Row 5 (RS): ch3, FPdc4tog over the next 4 dc, *1BPdc around the next 2 sts, (7dc) into the next st, 1BPdc around the next 2 sts, FPdc7tog over the next 7 sts*; repeat from * to * 4 more times, 1BPdc around the next 2 sts, 7dc into the next st, 1Bpdc around the next 2 sts, FPdc4tog, 1dc into the 3rd ch, turn.

First row of balloons completed.

Row 6 (WS): ch3, 1 BPdc around the next st, *1FPdc around the next 2 sts, 1BPdc around the next 7sts, 1FPdc around the next 2 sts, 1BPdc around the next st*; repeat from * to * 4 more times, 1FPdc around the next 2 sts, 1BPdc around the next 7 dc, 1FPdc around the next 2 sts, 1BPdc around the next st, 1dc into the 3rd ch, turn.

Row 7 (RS): ch3,1FPdc around the next st, *1BPdc around the next 2 sts, 1FPdc around the next 7 sts, 1BFPdc around the next 2 sts, 1FPdc around the next st*; repeat from * to * 4 more times, 1BPdc around the next 2 sts, 1FPdc around the next 7 sts, 1BPdc around the next 2 sts, 1FPdc around the next st, 1dc into the 3rd ch, turn.

Row 8 (WS): ch3, 1BPdc around the next st, *1FPdc around the next 2 sts, 1BPdc around the next 7 sts, 1FPdc around the next 2 sts, 1 BPdc around the next st*; repeat from * to * 4 more times, 1FPdc around the next 2 sts, 1BPdc around the next 7 dc, 1FPdc around the next 2 sts, 1BPdc around the next st, 1dc into the 3rd ch, turn.

Row 9 (RS): ch3, 4dc into the next st, *1BPdc around the next 2 sts, dc7tog over the next 7 sts, 1BPdc around the next 2 sts, 7dc into the next st*; repeat from * to * 4 more times, 1BPdc around the next 2 sts, dc7tog over the next 7 sts, 1BPdc around the next 2 sts, 4dc into the next st, 1dc into the 3rd ch.

Repeat Rows 2–9 another 4 more times for a total of 41 rows

Row 42 (WS): ch3, 1BPdc around the next 4 st,s *1FPdc around the next 2 sts, 1BPdc around the dc7tog, 1FPdc around the next 2 sts, 1BPdc around the next 7 sts*; repeat from * to * 4 more times, 1FPdc around the next 2 sts, 1BPdc around the next dc7tog, 1FPdc around the next 2 sts, 1BPdc around the next 4 sts, 1dc into the 3rd starting ch.

Cut yarn leaving a 1 AS length.

Block your finished front piece.

BACK

Join your contrast yarn to the last sc on Row 46, turn to WS.

Row 1 (RS): ch1, 1sc into each st to the end, turn. (75 sts)

Row 2 (WS): ch3, *dc2tog over the next 2 sts, 1dc into the next 10 sts*; repeat from * to * to last 2 sts, dc into last 2 sts, turn.

Row 3 (RS): ch3, dc to end. (69 sts)

Rows 4–30: repeat Row 3.

Fold up the two so the front panel is front side, facing the new back panel (so the piece is effectively inside out).

Row 31 (WS): Join to the chain from FRONT Row 1 and slip each stitch together with the cast-on st, skipping every 12th st of the Front row.

Cut yarn leaving a 1 AS length.

Using the 1 AS length thread the needle and blanket stitch down the side on one side (A).

Turn the piece outside in so the right side is now facing for the first panel. Insert your cushion filler. With the second 1 AS length sew the final opening closed with a blanket stitch. Sew in your ends.

MOSS STITCH blanket

A rectangular blanket is perfect for sharing. Wrap up with a special someone on a cold winter evening, or use it as a bed spread to wow your guests. It is a heavy and chunky blanket perfect for keeping warm while you crochet some more.

This blanket uses a simple moss stitch made from single crochet and chains to blend the colours together in a speckled look. Using two yarns together, the combination of a scrap cake with a solid contrast allows for a more muted look or a more vibrant vibe, depending on your choices!

YOU WILL NEED

YARN

1 x 300g (10½oz) Scrap cake
Use Scrap Cake 2 measurements from Scrap Cakes for Universal Projects.
Tip: You can split your scrap cake into two smaller cakes for ease of winding, Just remember to label them so you start with the right one!
300g (10½oz) ball of a contrast shade

HOOKS

o 6.5mm (K-10.5)
o 7mm (K-10.5 or L-11)

TOOLS AND NOTIONS

o Measuring tape
o Scissors
o Weighing scales
o Darning needle

MEASUREMENTS

81 x 76cm (32 x 30in)

TENSION (GAUGE)

8 sts (7 ch1sp) and 10 rows per 10cm (4in) square

PATTERN

Using a 6.5mm (K-10.5) hook.

Round 1 (RS): mr, *1sc into the mr, ch1*; repeat from * to * 9 more times, slst into first st to close, turn. (10 sc, 10 ch1sp)

Round 2 (WS): ch1, (1sc, ch2, 1sc, ch1). into the next ch1sp, (1sc, ch1) into each of the next 3 ch1sp, (1sc, ch2, 1sc, ch1) into the next ch1sp, (1sc, ch2, 1sc, ch1) into the next ch1sp, (1sc, ch1,) into the next 3 ch1sp, (1sc, ch2, 1sc, ch1) into the last ch1sp, slst into first st to close, turn. (14 sc, 14 ch1sp)

Round 3 (RS): ch1, sc into ch1sp below, ch1, *(1sc, ch2, 1sc, ch1) into corner ch2sp, (1sc, ch1) into each ch1sp to next ch2sp*; repeat from * to * another 2 times, (1sc, ch2, 1sc, ch1) into corner ch2sp, slst to first st to close, turn.

Round 4 (WS): ch1, (1sc, ch1) into each ch1sp to corner, *(1sc, ch2, 1sc, ch1) into corner ch2sp, (1sc, ch1) into each ch1sp to next ch2sp*; repeat from * to * another 2 times, (1sc, ch2, 1sc, ch1) into corner ch2sp, (1sc, ch1) into every ch1sp to start, slst to first st to close, turn.

Repeat Round 4 to end. Change to a slightly larger hook after Round 9.

Continue to desired size or until you run out of yarn. If you want a larger blanket after finishing your scrap cakes, continue working with longer lengths and changing colour whenever you feel like it.

BASKET
set

Baskets are one of the most useful household accessories. Store anything safely, from toys to your crochet projects; these baskets come in a range of sizes to fit all your needs.

This set of three basket-shaped project bags uses two strands at the same time. This makes for an easy-peasy quick project. Holding two scrap cakes double creates a more sporadic colour blending that works in ways you wouldn't have expected to match but really do work well. They are worked in a spiral so there is no turning throughout!

YOU WILL NEED

YARN

> **2 x 150g (5¼oz) Scrap cakes for each basket**
>
> Use Scrap Cake 3 measurements from Scrap Cakes for Universal Projects.

HOOKS

o 5mm (H-8)

TOOLS AND NOTIONS

o Measuring tape
o Scissors
o Weighing scales
o Stitch marker
o Darning needle

MEASUREMENTS

Basket 1: 40.5cm (16in) wide, base 25.5cm (10in)

Basket 2: 35.5cm (14in) wide, base 23cm (9in)

Basket 3: 30.5cm (12in) wide, base 20.5cm (8in)

TENSION (GAUGE)

13 sts and 9 rows per 10cm (4in) square over hdc pattern

SPECIAL ABBREVIATION

bl-hdc: work the hdc into the back loop of the stitch, the loop that's furthest away from you at the top of the stitch.

PATTERN

BASE

Round 1: mr, 4hdc into ring, pull ring closed. Do not join and work in an ongoing spiral. (5 sts)

Round 2: 2hdc into each st. (10 sts)

Place marker into the first hdc, move this marker up to the first st each round.

Round 3: 2hdc into the next 2 sts, *1hdc into the next st, 2hdc into the next st*; repeat from * to * 3 more times. (16 sts)

Round 4: *hdc into each st up to second st of each increase, 2hdc into second st of each increase*; repeat from * to * to end.

Repeat Round 4 another 5 (6, 7) times. (52 (58, 64) sts)

Next round: hdc, slst, ch1, turn.

SIDE

Round 1: bl-hdc into next st, bl-hdc into each st around. (52 (58, 64) sts)

Place marker into first hdc, move this marker up to the first st each round. Do not join and work in an ongoing spiral.

Repeat Round 1 another 10 times.

Round 12: *Work chainless foundation hdc into next st, then work a further 27 chainless foundation hdc, remove your hook and without twisting the ch, turn your chainless foundation into an 'O' shape, with RS still facing you, rejoin hook to work in the round and hdc into the first 5 sts of the chainless foundation, 2hdc into the next 2 sts, hdc into the next 4 sts, skip 10 sts of the basket, hdc into the next 15 (18, 21) sts*; repeat from * to * once more.

Cut yarn, leaving a long tail. Sew the lower part of the 'O' handle to the basket. Repeat for other handle using a small scrap of yarn.

HEXAGON
cardigan

Make your own fashion highlight using scrap cakes and the iconic granny stitch. This fabulous cardigan is super easy to make as each sleeve is made at the same time as half of the body, meaning you only need to join with some granny squares at the back and add all the borders!

You will need two scrap cakes for the sleeves but you can use any combination of random scraps for the eye-catching row of granny squares along the back, as well as the cuffs and hem. This allows you to pick colours that work best, to either create an extra pop of contrasting colours or to use something that matches. The choice is all yours!

YOU WILL NEED

YARN

2 x 155g (5½oz) Scrap cakes
Each scrap cake will require the following lengths:
1 x 100cm (40in)
1 x 153cm (60in)
1 x 216cm (85in)
3 x 2 AS
3 x 4 AS
3 x 5 AS
4 x 6 AS
4 x 8 AS
4 x 10 AS
5 x 12 AS
5 x 14 AS
5 x 16 AS
Note: These will be for the main body hexagons.
2 x 10 AS
Note: 1 per side to close up each side to create the sleeves
Multiple x 15g (½oz) scraps
Cuffs: Colours to match sleeves
Bottom Rib: Multiple colours
Edging: Multiple colours
Granny Squares: Multiple colours
Note: This section to finish the cardigan will be free range, where you can control your changing of the yarns. You will also use these for the granny squares, in whatever arrangement you prefer.

HOOKS
o 5mm (H-8)
o 6mm (J-10)

TOOLS AND NOTIONS
o Measuring tape
o Scissors
o Weighing scales
o 4 stitch markers
o Darning needle

MEASUREMENTS
65cm (25½in) across from underarm to underarm

63.5cm (25in) top to bottom

35.5cm (14in) sleeve length

137cm (54in) cuff to cuff

Each granny square measures 12.5cm (5in) along each side

TENSION (GAUGE)
5 trio repeats and 8 rows per 10cm (4in) square

SPECIAL ABBREVIATIONS
trio: 3dc in same space (granny stitch)
picot: ch5, slst into the first ch to form a loop
BLBB: Back Loop and Back Bump

PATTERN

SLEEVES AND BODY

Round 1: mr, stsc into the mr, 2dc, ch2, *3dc into the mr, ch2*; repeat 5 more times. slst into top of the stsc to close. (18 sts, 6 ch2sp).

Round 2: stsc into the chsp previously worked (behind your slst), *ch1, 3dc into the next ch2sp, ch2, 3dc into the same ch2sp*; repeat from * to * 4 more times, ch1, 3dc into the remaining ch2sp, ch2, 2dc into the same space, slst into the stsc to close. (36 sts, 6 ch2sp, 6 ch1sp).

Round 3: slst into the next ch1, (stsc, 2dc) into the same space, *ch1, (3dc, ch2, 3dc) into the next ch2sp, ch1, 3dc into the next ch1sp, ch1*; repeat 4 more times, slst into the stsc to close.

Repeat Rounds 2 and 3 consecutively until you have a total of 23 rounds.

Next Round: work up to the point you have half a round/side made up. Your finishing point should be halfway between corners. You will have two full sides to go, as well as the half side you are currently working and the remaining section to the beginning of the round.

Attach your 1 x 10 AS. Continue the side you are on. Stop at the next corner (A).

Fold the piece from one corner to the opposite corner making the piece an irregular hexagon shape, making sure the side unworked is flush with the opposite side (B).

Start the joining of the sides with the corner. Work 3dc into the ch2sp corner on the working side. ch1, slst into the opposite corner ch2sp. Finish the corner with a second set of 3dc into the ch2sp of the working side. slst into the ch1sp after the opposite side's corner. *Work up the side as normal, but use a slst into the opposite ch1sp after each trio of dc (this replaces the ch1 between trios)*; repeat the side from * to *. Then repeat this paragraph starting with the next corner so you have joined two sides. Finish working the remaining side to the beginning of the round.

Work the second sleeve in the same way.

(B)

(A)

Your hexagon will not be lying flat as you make it.

Don't worry!

This is normal and means that you will be able to fold it into the L-shape needed.

GRANNY SQUARES

Once you have 2 identical pieces worked up you can move onto making the granny squares to join the back sections together. Lay both sleeve sections flat with back facing up, use stitch markers to indicate the back top and bottom corners on each side. These are your joining corners.

Following the granny square instructions (see Square Variations: Granny Square), work up 4 rounds. Start Round 5 and stop at the first corner. For the next side, repeat the instructions from * to * used for joining the sleeves to join the granny square to the sleeve pieces starting at the bottom right joining corner (C).

Complete the next side and corner and attach the 3rd side to the second back section, starting after the 5th trio up from the stitch marker using the same joining method. Complete the corner and finish the remaining side to close with a slst into the stsc.

For the next 3 squares, start attaching on Round 5 of the granny square In the same way. At the first corner, join to the left side of the sleeve piece, after the 5th trio up from the previous granny square

join. The next side will be joined to the previous granny square, followed by joining the next side to the right side of the back. Finish the granny square in the usual way.

Work four Granny Squares in this manner.

At the last square if you have a row or two of the sleeve pieces remaining unattached, this can be filled with rows of trios using the same attachment technique used to join the squares. Once the shoulders are flush, close with a slst.

CUFFS (MAKE 2)

Join a 15g (½oz) scrap to the corner with the slst made for the closure of the arms, by pulling up the yarn under the slst, and attach with a ch1.

Round 1: stsc into the same space, *3dc into the next ch1sp*; repeat from * to * until the last ch1sp BEFORE the corner ch2sp. Working over the tail from the stsc, work 1dc into the corner ch2sp, dc2tog working both into the same ch2sp and the first ch2sp together. slst into the stsc.

Round 2: slst into the next space between the trios, stsc into the same space, 2dc into the same space, *3dc

into the space between the next trio*; repeat from * to * to the last space of the round, slst top of stsc to close.

Round 3: ch1, 1 sc2tog into the st below and over the next st, *1sc over the next 2 sts, sc2tog over the next 2 sts*; repeat from, * to * to last st, 1sc into last st, slst to close.

Round 4: repeat Round 3.

Round 5: stsc into the st below, 1dc into each st to the last st, slst to close.

Round 6: 1FPstsc around the first dc post below, *1BPdc around the next dc post, 1FPdc around the next dc post*; repeat from * to * to last st, BPdc around last dc, slst into the first stsc to close.

Round 7: 1FPstsc around the FPdc below, *1BPdc around the BPdc below. 1FPdc around the FPdc below*; repeat from * to * to last stitch, BPdc, slst into the top of the stsc to close.

Round 8: repeat Round 7.

Round 9: BLBBsc into each st, slst into the first sc to close, ch1.

Cut yarn here.

FRONT EDGING

Lay the cardigan flat facing you. Start on the bottom corner of the right side. Switch up yarns as you choose for a freehand scrappy look.

Round 1: Join any yarn to corner, *3dc into the ch1sp, ch1*; repeat from * to * along bottom edge (F). For the joins between granny squares and the body, work the trio as: 1dc into first ch2sp, dc2tog into the first and second ch2sp, dc into second ch2sp.

When you reach the first corner, work 3dc, ch2, 2sc into that ch2sp.

Along the side, work 1sc into each st and ch1sp. For the back and neck join, work a sc2tog into the two ch2sp. Continue in the same manner working 1sc into each st and ch1sp along the neck. Work another sc2tog into the next back and neck join. Then work 1sc into each st and ch1sp along the next side.

Once you reach the bottom ch2sp, work 2sc into the ch2sp, slst to join.

Round 2: ch1, 3dc into the same ch2sp, *3dc into the ch1sp*; repeat from * to * to the next corner, (3dc, ch2, 1dc) into the ch2sp, 1dc into each stitch up to the neck, around the neck and down the right side to the next corner ch2sp, (2dc, ch2, 3dc) into the ch2sp.

Round 3: (3dc, 1sc) into the side of the last dc just worked, 1sc into the bottom section of the same dc, 1sc into each st until the next ch2sp, 2sc, ch2, 3dc into the ch2sp, *3dc in between each set of 3dc*; repeat from * to * to the next corner ch2sp (G).

Round 4: slst into the top of the sc, picot, *slst across the front post of the next 4 sts, picot*; repeat from * to * until you reach the next ch2sp, slst into the first ch, picot, sc2tog to the first picot made, slst into the ch2sp behind the picot (H–J).

Round 5: stsc, dc into the same ch2sp *dc into the sts from Round 3*; repeat from * to * to the next ch2sp, 2dc, ch2, 2dc, repeat from * to * to the next ch2sp, 2dc, ch2, slst into the stsc to close.

Round 6: 1sc into each st to the next ch2sp, 1sc, 1hdc, 1dc into the ch2sp, *FPdc around next st, BPdc around next st*; repeat from * to * to the next ch2sp, 1dc, 1hdc, 1sc into the next ch2sp, slst into the first sc to close.

If your gauge/tension varies a bit and your edging feels too loose and wavy or too tight, change your hook to one size smaller or larger and try again.

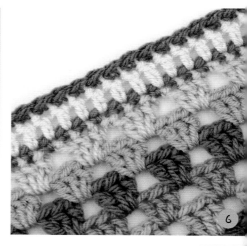

Round 7: BLslst into each st to the next ch2sp, slst into the ch, ch3, 1dc into the ch2sp, work FPdc and BPdc according to set pattern to last st.

Rows 8 and 9 are worked only along the bottom edge in Rows.

Row 8: Switch yarns to the yarn colour used for the cuffs, stsc, work FPdc and BPdc according to the set pattern to end.

Row 9: Repeat Row 8.

Sew in your ends and block to desired measurements.

Notes

To work a larger jumper, work extra rows along edges 1 and 3 of your hexagon. These will be the front and back edges. Then, seam the shoulders as described, working into the sides of the starting dc of the extra rows. This will add extra width around the bust. Do the same on each hexagon. Working 2 rows extra on two edges of each hexagon will add 10cm (4in) to the bust circumference / 5cm (2in) to the measurement from underarm to underarm.

GENERAL TECHNIQUES

MAGIC RING

This is an alternative to a chain ring; it can be tightened to leave a much smaller central hole.

1. Wrap the yarn a couple of times around your two middle fingers and hold it securely with your thumb (A).

2. Insert your hook in the loop and catch the ball-end of the yarn (B).

3. Pull it through and make a chain stitch to secure. Make the first round of stitches into the loop (C).

4. Pull the yarn tail to tighten the loop (D).

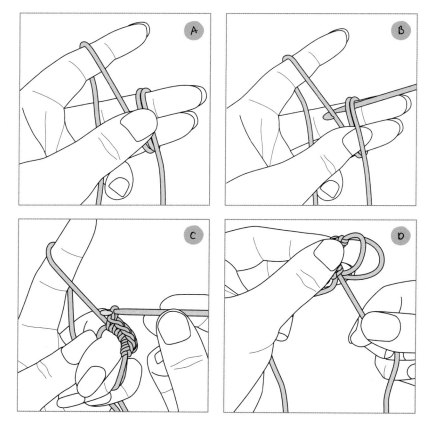

CHAINLESS FOUNDATION

Working a chainless foundation is a quicker way to work the first row of any project that requires a row start, for example a blanket. Always start with a slip knot, then continue depending on the stitch required.

SINGLE CROCHET CHAINLESS FOUNDATION

1. Chain 2.

2. Insert your hook into the 2nd chain from the hook.

3. *Ch1 (make note of this chain – use a marker if required).

4. Yarn over and pull through 2 loops (A).

5. Insert hook into ch1* (the base of the previous sc) (B).

6. Repeat from * to * until you reach the desired stitch count (C).

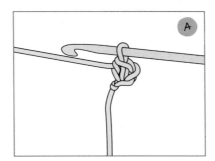

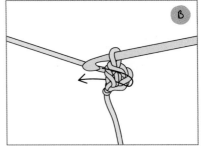

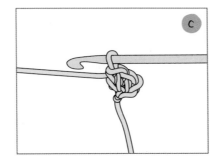

DOUBLE CROCHET CHAINLESS FOUNDATION

1. Chain 3.

2. Yarn over, insert your hook into the 3rd chain from the hook.

3. *Ch1 (make note of this chain – use a marker if required) (A).

4. Yarn over and pull through 2 loops.

5. Yarn over and pull through 2 loops again (B).

6. Insert hook into ch1* (the base of the previous dc) (C).

7. Repeat from * to * until you reach the desired stitch count (D).

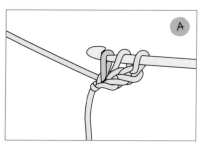
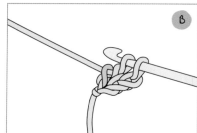
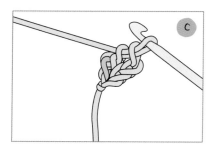
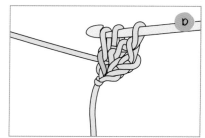
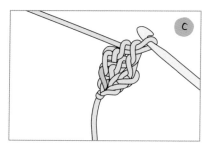

HALF DOUBLE CROCHET CHAINLESS FOUNDATION

1. Chain 2.

2. Yarn over, insert your hook into the 2nd chain from the hook.

3. *Ch1 (make note of this chain – use a marker if required) (A).

4. Yarn over and pull through 3 loops (B).

5. Insert hook into ch1* (the base of the previous hdc) (C).

6. Repeat from * to * for desired stitch count (D).

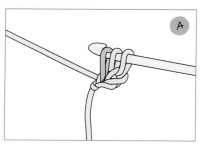
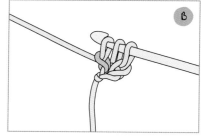

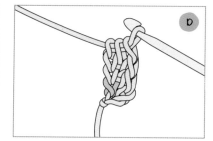

OTHER STITCHES

STACKED SINGLE CROCHET

Working a stacked single crochet always looks much neater and is easier to find to work stitches into. Beginning the row with a stsc doesn't require a ch1 to start either.

1. Insert your hook into the first stitch on the new row (if working in the round the first st is the same stitch previously slip stitched from the row below) (A).

2. Work a sc into this stitch (remember, don't ch1!) (B).

3. Insert the hook into the front bar of the sc just made and work another sc the same way (C).

4. The two sc are stacked one on top of the other, creating the same height as a dc (D).

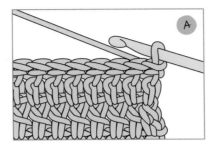
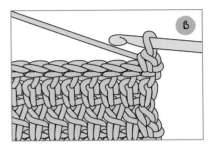
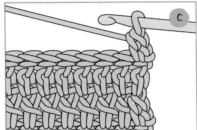
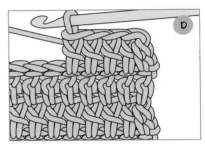

STACKED TREBLE

A stacked treble is worked using the same principle as stacked single crochet, but working trebles.

PUFF STITCH

1. Yarn over, insert your hook into the stitch.

2. Pull up a loop through the stitch (3 loops on your hook) (A).

3. Yarn over, insert hook into the same stitch.

4. Pull up a loop through the stitch (5 loops on your hook) (B).

5. Yarn over, insert hook into the same stitch.

6. Pull up a loop through the stitch (7 loops on your hook) (C).

7. Yarn over and pull through all 7 loops (D).

8. Chain 1 (E).

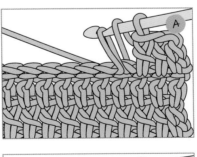
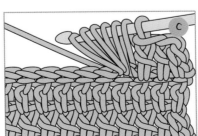
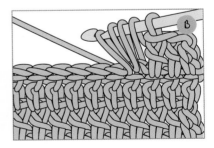
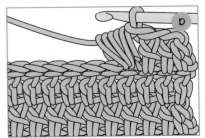

NO TAIL METHOD

We all hate sewing in our tails and ends after finishing a project so here is a technique I use to join a new yarn to a piece without having tails dangling off to sew in later.

1. Work the stitches up to the point you need to switch yarns.

2. Leave your hook in place and the tension how you would have it when wanting to continue. Carefully cut the yarn about 0.5cm (¼in) from the hook, under the last st just worked and pinch the tail (A).

3. Hold tail securely and remove your hook from the loop.

4. Pull the tail to unravel a few stitches (B).

5. Magic knot the new yarn to the tail, leaving a very small tail for the unravelled yarn (C).

6. Rework those stitches again. (D–E)

The knot should now sit neatly in the last stitch, if not then rework making sure that your tension is as it was before. Continue with the pattern and hey presto you have no tails!

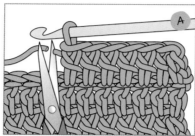
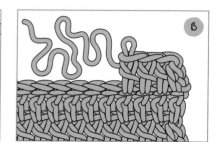

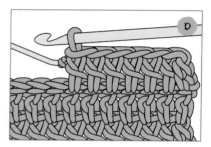
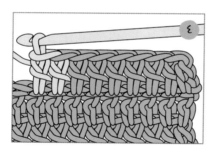

CLUSTER STITCH

1. Yarn over, insert your hook in a stitch and pull up a loop, yarn over and pull through 2 loops (2 loops on hook), yarn over and insert your hook in the same stitch (A).

2. Pull up a loop, yarn over and pull through 2 loops (3 loops on hook), yarn over and pull through all loops (B).

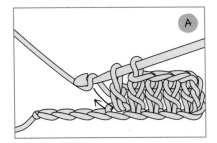
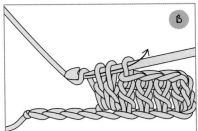

FRONT AND BACK POST DOUBLE CROCHET

1. Yarn over and insert your hook around the post of the next stitch, from the back for a back post dc (A) and from the front for a fount post dc (C).

2. Pull up a loop and finish your dc as usual (B and D).

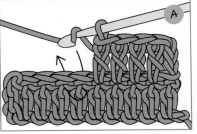
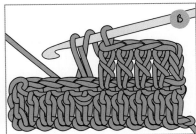
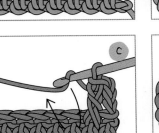
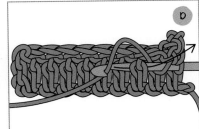

SQUARE VARIATIONS

Scrap cakes can work with any project and these squares could give you some ideas. The moss stitch can be worked as an ever-expanding square or you can work individual granny squares and piece them together. Give these variations a go to see what inspires you.

MOSS STITCH SQUARE

Use Scrap Cake 1 (see Scrap Cakes for Universal Projects).

Round 1: mr, *(sc, ch2) into the ring*; repeat from * to * 3 more times, slst into sc to close, turn.

Round 2: *(sc, ch2, sc) into next ch2sp, ch1*; repeat from * to * 3 more times, slst into sc to close, turn.

Round 3: *sc into next ch1sp, ch1, (sc, ch2, sc) into ch2sp, ch1*; repeat from * to * 3 more times, slst into sc to close, turn.

Round 4: *(sc, ch1) into each ch1sp to corner, (sc, ch2, sc, ch1) into corner ch2sp*; repeat from * to * 3 more times, (sc, ch1) into each ch1sp to start, slst into sc to close, turn.

Repeat Round 4 until desired size.

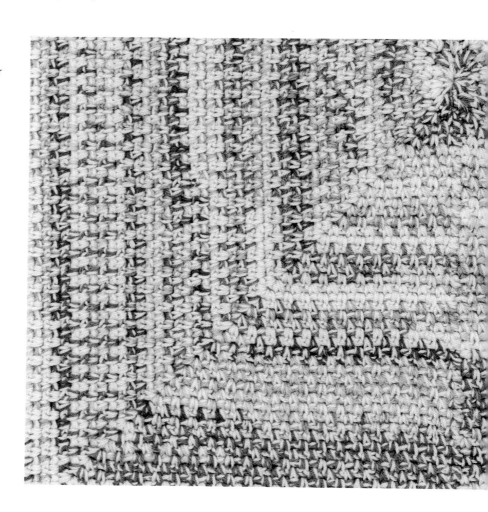

GRANNY SQUARE

Use Scrap Cake 2 (see Scrap Cakes for Universal Projects).

Round 1: mr, stsc into the ring, 2dc into the ring, ch2, *3dc into the ring, ch2*; repeat from * to * 2 more times, slst into the top of the stsc to close, turn.

Round 2: stsc into ch2sp, 2dc into the same space, (ch2sp, ch2, 3dc) into the same ch2sp, *(3dc, ch2, 3dc) into the next ch2sp*; repeat from * to * 2 more times, slst into the top of the stsc, turn.

Round 3: stsc into the space below (between the sets of 3 dc), 2dc into the same space, *(3dc, ch2, 3dc) into the next ch2sp, 3dc into the space between the trios*; repeat from * to * 2 more times, (3dc, ch2, 3dc) into ch2sp, slst into the top of the stsc to close, turn.

Round 4: stsc into the space below, 2dc into the same space, *(3dc, ch2, 3dc) into ch2sp, 3dc into each space between the trios to next corner*; repeat from * to * another 2 times, (3dc, ch2, 3dc) into ch2sp, 3dc into each space between the trios to beginning, slst into the top of the stsc to close, turn.

Round 5: stsc into the space below, 2dc into the same space, *3dc into each space between the trios to corner, (3dc, ch2, 3dc) into ch2sp*; repeat from * to * another 3 times, 3dc into each space between the trios to start, slst into the top of the stsc to close, turn.

Repeat Round 5 as often as desired.

SPECIAL ABBREVIATIONS

trio: 3dc in same space (granny stitch)

ABOUT THE AUTHOR

My name is Naomi, and I live in the southwest of Dorset. I have spent the past 20 years raising my family and finding my creative feet. This has led me from hosting art exhibitions to local craft fairs, cake design, and finally crochet. By a small fluke, I found a crochet hook in an old bag of knitting needles that had belonged to my grandmother. I looked up crochet and the world of crochet opened up for me.

Art has been my passion since I could hold a crayon and my only path through life has been creative and colourful. With every area of art I have explored, it has always been primarily about colour and secondly about reusing things I had to hand. When raising a small army of kids, there is only loose change to spend on hobbies. Instead, I relied on what I had to hand at the time. Then I could proceed to creating and making things for actual customers who, to my surprise, really did love the things I created. Whether I was armed with a paint brush, cakes, fondant, or yarn, I found a niche that would help propel me into the market for a few sales! And the best part: I loved what I could do!

Colour has always been my therapy. I believe colour is our most important supporter and protector in everything we do. Colours make us happy and warm and everyone has a particular colour they warm to the most. We need to embrace the colours we love best, to help us focus and manage our way through a busy life. We choose a colour palette for our clothing and for our homes. These colours show us what our passions are.

I have had so much encouragement throughout my life, to progress and explore my creativity, especially from my parents. They are most definitely my biggest cheerleaders!

ACKNOWLEDGEMENTS

One person I have to dedicate this book to is my husband. He has supported my art endeavours over the 20 years we have had our small family. Whatever project, subject or medium I have wanted to pursue, he has always been the one who held me up whenever I needed it. He is also the one who dashed out to the store for last minute icing to finish a wedding cake and patiently waits for me to explore any new-to-me yarn store we find.

INDEX

abbreviations 10
arm spans 15, 22–3

back post crochet (bp) 10, 80, 107
bags
    hessian bag cover 36–9
    tulip tote 46–9
balloon stitch 80–1
basket set 88–91
blanket
    corner to corner 58–61
    Dave's 54–7
    granny square 66–9
    moss stitch 84–7
    working/yarn required 16

cardigan, hexagon 92–9
chainless foundation 103–4
circular crochet, scrap cakes 17, 29
cluster stitch (cl) 107
clutch purse 74–9
colours
    altering 14
    changing 16–17, 106
    contrast shade 19
    creating colourway 18–21
    inspiration 21
    planning 16, 18, 20–1
conversion tables 10
corner to corner blanket 58–61
cowl 62–5
crochet hooks 8, 10
cushion, balloon pillow 80–3

double crochet (dc)
    chainless foundation row 104
    front/back post 10, 107
double crochet (UK) see single
    crochet
foundation row, chainless 103–4
front post crochet (fp) 10, 80, 107

getting started 14–17
granny square
    blanket 66–9
    in hexagon cardigan 92
    magic ring start 102
    measuring yarn 17
    scrap cakes 17, 29
    square variations 109

half-double crochet (hdc), chainless
    foundation 104
half-treble crochet (UK) see half-
    double crochet
hexagon cardigan 92–9

labels 14, 27

magic knot 24–5
magic ring (mr) 102
materials 8
measuring tape 8, 14
moss stitch
    blanket 84–7
    square variation 108

needles 8

pillow, balloon 80–3
pompom maker 8
pot cover 70–3
projects
    balloon pillow 80–3
    basket set 88–91
    clutch purse 74–9
    corner to corner blanket 58–61
    cowl 62–5
    Dave's blanket 54–7
    granny square blanket 66–9
    hessian bag cover 36–9
    hexagon cardigan 92–9
    moss stitch blanket 84–7
    pot cover 70–3
    scrap cakes 29
    snood 32–5
    sunshine wrap 40–5
    triangle puff shawl 50–3
puff stitch (ps) 105
    snood 32
    triangular shawl 50

random cakes 14
rows, projects worked in
    chainless foundation 103–4
    Dave's blanket 54–7
    getting started 16
    measuring yarn 16
    scrap cakes 29

scissors 8

scrap cakes 6, 12
    making 22–3, 28–9
    weighing 23
shawl
    sunshine wrap 40–5
    triangle puff 50–3
single crochet (sc)
    chainless foundation 103
    stacked 105
snood 32–5
square projects
    hessian bag cover 36–9
    moss stitch blanket 84–7
    scrap cakes 17, 29
    variations 108–9
    see also granny squares
stacked single crochet (stsc) 105
stitch markers 8
stitches
    abbreviations 10
    techniques 103–7
swatch, making 19

tape measure 8, 14
techniques 102–9
theme, choosing 20
tools 8
treble crochet (UK) see double
    crochet
triangular projects
    estimating yarn 17
    puff shawl 50–3
    sunshine wrap 40–5

UK/US terms 10

weighing scales 8
wrap, sunshine 40–5

yarn 8
    amount required 14
    cutting lengths 15–17
    joining 24–5
    measuring lengths 22–3
    no tail join 106
    organising 6, 14
    used double 19, 46, 54, 84, 88
    weighing 23
yarn bowl 8
yarn winders 6, 8, 26–7

A catalogue record for this book is available from the
British Library.

ISBN-13: 9781446313626 paperback
ISBN-13: 9781446313640 EPUB
ISBN-13: 9781446313633 PDF

This book has been printed on paper from approved
suppliers and made from pulp from sustainable sources.

FSC
www.fsc.org

MIX
Paper | Supporting
responsible forestry
FSC® C136333

Printed in China through Asia Pacific Offset for:
David and Charles, Ltd
Suite A, Tourism House, Pynes Hill, Exeter, EX2 5WS

10 9 8 7 6 5 4 3 2 1

Publishing Director: Ame Verso
Senior Commissioning Editor: Sarah Callard
Editor: Jessica Cropper
Project Editor: Sam Winkler
Head of Design: Anna Wade
Designers: Anna Wade, Lee-May Lim and Jess Pearson
Pre-press Designer: Susan Reansbury
Illustrations: Kuo Kang Chen
Art Direction: Sarah Rowntree
Photography: Jason Jenkins
Production Manager: Beverley Richardson

David and Charles publishes high-quality books on
a wide range of subjects. For more information visit
www.davidandcharles.com.

Share your makes with us on social media using
#dandcbooks and follow us on Facebook and
Instagram by searching for @dandcbooks.

Layout of the digital edition of this book may vary
depending on reader hardware and display settings.